The World, The Flesh, and The Devil

The World, The Flesh, and The Devil

*

Practical Insight to Living Victoriously In Christ

Written by Roderick L. Evans

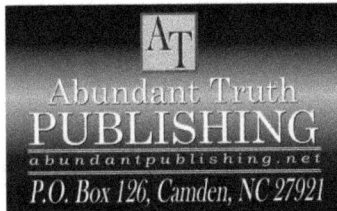

Aᴛ
Abundant Truth
PUBLISHING
abundantpublishing.net
P.O. Box 126, Camden, NC 27921

The World, The Flesh, and The Devil
Practical Insights to Living Victoriously in Christ

Front & Back Cover Designs by Abundant Truth Publishing
Image by Flavio Takemoto/www.takemote.com.br
www.sxc.hu

Abundant Truth Publishing
an imprint of Abundant Truth International Ministries

For information address:
Abundant Truth International
P.O. Box 126
Camden, NC 27921

Unless otherwise indicated, all of the scripture quotations are taken from the *Authorized King James Version* of the Bible. Scripture quotations marked with NIV are taken from the *New International Version* of the Bible. Scripture quotations marked with NASV are taken from the *New American Standard Version* of the Bible. Scripture quotations marked with Amplified are taken from the *Amplified Bible*.

ISBN 13: 978-1-60141-000-9

Printed in the United States of America.

Contents

Preface

Living a Christian life in today's society has become increasingly difficult. Believers must strive daily to live as God has ordained. The condition in which the world is in is quite evident; for we need only to turn to television and newspapers for a clear picture of the times that we are living in. People have lost respect for one another. Murder and rapes occur every minute. Those in government positions are constantly involved in scandals. In addition, society as a whole, disregards the fear of God and His statutes.

So then, how can the believer live in this world without compromise?

How can Christians live in a world that is opposed to Christ and His teachings?

If we have become the children of God through the new birth in Christ, we now have the strength to overcome the world. Our faith in God gives us the victory. Still, faith alone does not guarantee success. Unless accompanied by some type of action, failure can still be the result. James 2:17 illustrates this point, "Even so faith, if it has no works, is dead, being by itself."

Conversely, when action follows true faith, it will result in the believer living a victorious life in Christ. It is essential that we first operate in faith before taking any action. Once our faith in God is established, we must acquire the steps needed to conquer the three areas that plague the Christian life most: **the world, the flesh, and the devil.** It is our prayer that the simple, practical truths presented will help you live in victory.

Roderick L. Evans

Introduction

The Bible is filled with commandments and exhortations encouraging the believer to be holy and to separate himself from the world. Christ referred to Christians as lights and declared that they have power over the devil; yet without question, the enemy dominates many believers.

Believers and non-believers, alike, have the wrong concept of the enemy. They think domination by the enemy means someone is possessed. We think about the movie, The Exorcist, where the girl's face changes color and she spews up green slime. The media has shaped our view rather than the scriptures.

The scriptures let us know that the enemy's control is not always easily recognized. We must realize that the enemy fights and gains control in a person's life in a subtle way. He fights using man's own sinful nature against himself. If we do not overcome our sinful nature, we cannot effectively fight against him.

> *If you have raced with the men on foot and they have worn you out, how wan you compete with horses? If you stumble in safe country, how will you manage in the thickets by the Jordan? (Jeremiah 12:5 NIV)*

The prophet Jeremiah asked his listeners a question: if they could not last while racing ordinary men, how could they compete with horses? His point was that if you cannot handle the things that are going on now, what about when things get worse. In essence, the believer must ask similar questions: If you have not come out of the world, how can you gain control over your flesh? In addition, if you have not gained the victory over your flesh, how can you face and defeat the enemy? Finally, if you cannot walk in victory over the enemy, how can you live a victorious Christian life?

Overcoming the world, the flesh, and the devil is a process. You must move from one area to the next. You must first overcome the world, so that you will be able to conquer the desires of the flesh. And once the desires of the flesh are crucified, you will be able to face the adversary. After overcoming the schemes and tactics of the enemy, you can live victoriously in

Christ.

In order to have dominion over the world, the flesh, and the devil, we need only to follow examples set forth in God's Word, observing both Old and New Testament guidelines. Christians who rely solely on New Testament teachings while neglecting Old Testament scriptures run the risk of missing valuable lessons. Paul says the scriptures were written for our encouragement.

> *For whatever was written in earlier times was written for our instruction, that through perseverance and the encouragement of the scriptures, we might have hope. (Romans 15:4)*

He takes up this theme again when he says the events that happened unto the Israelites were written for our instruction.

Now these things happened unto them as an example, and they were written for our instruction, upon whom the ends of the ages have come. (I Corinthians 10:11)

Therefore, we must not ignore the Old Testament scriptures. In addition, we recognize that it is through the Old Testament scriptures, as Paul says, that we learn by example to have patience. This should encourage us and give us hope.

We will now look at examples for the Old and New Testaments that will help us to understand the process needed to gain victory over the world, the flesh, and the devil. Our Old Testament example will be the Jews.

Israel

The book of Exodus introduces us to the nation of Israel who is bondage in Egypt. Egypt, at this time, was one of the most powerful and influential nations in the world. The pharaohs had enslaved them for over 400 years. The Egyptian empire forced them to be laborers. Their masters placed heavy burdens upon them daily. Because of this, they began to cry out to God.

It was during this time that God appeared to Moses. He told him that he had heard the cries of Israel and that He would deliver them. Armed with God's name, Moses relay's God's command to Pharaoh: "Let My People Go!" After multiple signs and wonders, Pharaoh submits and urges Israel to leave Egypt.

Upon Israel's departure, God leads them through the Red Sea into the wilderness. They were on their way to Canaan, the land of promise. While in the wilderness, God tested them. They failed these tests. Therefore, they did not go directly into Canaan, but were forced to wander in the wilderness for a total of 40 years. It was only after this time were the Israelites able to fight against the inhabitants of Canaan and enter into the Promised Land.

Let us now examine the process of the Israelites. Before they could go to Canaan, they had to first leave Egypt. Egypt was a nation that the whole world looked upon. It was the ideal nation of its time. It serves as a representation of the world. Israel, figuratively, had to come out of the world.

Before Moses could lead them out, the people had to get rid of the Egyptian idols that were in their possessions. They had to set themselves apart from any Egyptian influence that was present in their worship of God. Not only were they to leave Egypt physically, but its influences also.

Next, we find that God did not take them directly to Canaan. God gives them this reason,

> *And you shall remember all the way in which the Lord God has led you in the wilderness these forty years, that he might humble you, testing you, to know what was in your heart, whether you would keep His commandments or not. (Deuteronomy 8:2)*

God kept them from the Promised Land in order to teach them how to obey His commands. He wanted the Israelites to have control, even in their flesh. There are numerous incidents recorded of how the Israelites allowed fleshly desires to control them. They complained when they had no food; they complained when they had no meat; they complained when they had no water, and so on.

While in the wilderness, He gave them the commandments. These were given to set boundaries on their desires and to separate them from the other nations. Here, we see that the Israelites had to bring their fleshly desires under control before they could go into Canaan.

We should note here that after three years in the wilderness, God brought Israel to Kadesh-Barnea. The only thing they had to do was to fight and enter. They failed. Because they had not fully surrendered themselves to God, they would not believe Him for the victory. Therefore, when they tried to face their enemy to enter into the Promised

Land, they were defeated. This is why they stayed in the wilderness for 37 more years – to learn to obey and trust God. Though it took years, Israel finally learned what was necessary.

After a total of 40 years, Israel returned to Canaan. They were prepared to confront their enemies and win. They fought battle after battle with success. After years of fighting, God gave them rest and they were able to live in the land of promise.

Looking at Israel, we see that God took them through the process: first, they had to come out of the world (leave Egypt); second, they had to gain control over their flesh (God gave them the commandments and caused them to wander until they walked in obedience); and finally, they had to face the enemy (they had to fight the inhabitants of Canaan).

After they overcame these three areas, they could live victoriously (God gave them rest because all the land was subdued before them). If we follow their example, we too can live an undefeated life in Christ.

Jesus

To find an example in the New Testament, we need to only look to Jesus. He is the example that every Christian should follow. After John baptized Him and the Spirit anointed Him, Jesus was led into the wilderness. In order for Him to go into the wilderness, He had to leave the inhabited places. This was significant because it shows that there was a separation from the rest of the world.

When a person gives his heart to Christ, the Holy Spirit will cause him to be separate from the rest of the world. Jesus set an example for all believers to follow: total separation from the world. Jesus gained the victory over the world because He showed a willingness to leave it behind in order to commune with God. Through this victory, He could move on to the next area to conquer – the flesh.

And after he had fasted forty days and forty nights, he then became hungry. (Matthew 4:2)

Jesus disciplined himself through fasting. Fasting is a discipline wherein a believer denies his carnal appetites. Through fasting and prayer, the believer gains control over his flesh. After fasting for forty days and nights, Jesus brought His flesh under control and conquered it. Having overcome the world through separation and conquering the flesh through fasting, Jesus was prepared to face the final challenge – the devil.

And the tempter (devil) came and said to him, "If you are the son of God, command that these stones become bread." But he answered and said, "It is written, 'Man shall not live by bread alone, but on every word that proceeds out of the mouth of God. (Matthew 4:3-4 Parenthesis mine)

In these verses, we find Jesus being confronted by the tempter (devil). He is also found using the most effective weapon available to defeat the enemy – the Word. With every tactic the enemy used, Jesus continually fought and conquered with the Word. Jesus used the Word to defeat the enemy again and again.

Then the devil took him into the holy city; and he had him stand on the pinnacle of the temple, and said unto him, "If you are the son of God throw yourself down; for it is written, 'he will give his angels charge concerning you and on their hands they will bear you up, lest you strike your foot against a stone.' Jesus said unto him, "On the other hand, it is written, 'you shall not put the Lord your God to the test.' Again, the devil took him to a very high mountain, and showed him all the kingdoms of the world, and their glory; and said unto him, "All these things will I give you, if you will fall down and worship me." Then Jesus said unto him, "Be gone, Satan! For it is written, 'you shall worship the Lord your God and serve him only.' (Matthew 4:5-10)

It is through this example that we learn the most vital information. By using the Word, Jesus rebuked the devil. He told him to leave (Matthew 4:10). Thus, to defeat the devil, the believer must study the Word and understand how to use it as a weapon against the enemy. After effectively using the Word, the enemy could no longer stand against Jesus, and was defeated.

Then the devil left him, and behold, angels came and began to minister to him. (Matthew 4:11)

After these events, we find Jesus entering into His public ministry with great power and results. He conquered all three areas and went on to live a life of victory. Every Christian can follow this pattern.

As we shall discover later on in this book, we can also follow Jesus' example through very practical steps. Not only should the believer read and pray, but there are also steps to take in everyday life to overcome the world, the flesh, and the devil. The steps that we take to overcome must be based upon spiritual principles, or else we will fail.

> *For our struggle is not against flesh and blood, but against the rulers, against the authorities, against the powers of this dark world, and against spiritual forces of evil in the heavenly realms. (Ephesians 6:12 NIV)*

Though our struggle may manifest in the flesh, its origin is from the spirit realm. It is evident that God created man as flesh and blood, but because of the weaknesses of our flesh, we cannot fight in the flesh. We must operate in the power of the Spirit. Paul goes further by saying,

> *For though we walk in the flesh, we do not war according to the flesh. (II Corinthians 10:3)*

Since we cannot fight with our own natural abilities, we must use spiritual weapons and spiritually based strategies if we are to conquer the world, the flesh, and the devil.

Section 1

▼

The World

Do not love the world, nor the things that are in the world. I John 2:15a

The world is designed to cater to the desires of man. The Apostle John exhorts his readers not to love the things that are in the world. The scriptures continue this theme by stating that where our treasure is, our heart will be there also (Matthew 6:21). Therefore, if we love the things that the world has to offer, our devotion will be towards the world and not towards Christ. God gives us all things to enjoy freely, but they are not to become our motivation for living.

The Word of God commands believers to separate themselves from the world. We usually

1

think coming out of the world means parting with old friends and not associating with unbelievers. This is only partially true. To be separate from the world means to be free from its influence and control also.

In both the Old and New Testaments, the command of God to His people was that they be unique, different, and set aside for Him. Therefore, in its simplest form, God's command tells us that in order to serve Him fully; there must be a separation, which is to be spiritual and/or physical. This, however, does include family members. Jesus said,

> *Do not think that I came to bring peace on earth; I did not come to bring peace, but a sword. For I came to set a man against his father, and a daughter against her mother, and a daughter-in-law against her mother-in-law; and a man's foes will be the*

members of this household. (Matthew 10:34-36)

He also stated,

If any man comes to me, and does not hate his own father and mother and wife and children and brothers and sisters, yes, even his own life, he cannot be my disciple. (Luke 14:26)

Jesus is not instructing us to hate our families. He makes it clear that the believer must not love anyone, even himself, above God.

Christians, for centuries, have debated what is considered to be "of the world," or "worldly." Many people sometimes suggest that the Bible is too vague when it speaks of not being of the "world." We have all heard people say, "The Bible does not say you can't dance. It does not say that you cannot smoke. If it does not say it, it does not matter." This is simply not an excuse to indulge in ungodliness.

Before going into scripture, we must establish a definition of "worldliness." Worldliness or worldly, simply put, refers to the world's system or the world's way of doing things. To be "in the world," the believer must still behave as those who are in the world. If the believer does not correct his mentality, his lifestyle will begin to mirror those who are in the world. Those caught in the world's system are individuals who live only to please themselves. II Timothy 3:2-5 describes these types of people,

> *For men will be lovers of self, lovers of money, boastful, arrogant, revilers, disobedient to parents, ungrateful, unholy, unloving, irreconcilable, malicious gossips, without self-control, brutal, haters of good,*

treacherous, reckless, conceited, lovers of pleasure rather than lovers of God; holding to a form of godliness, although they have denied its power; and avoid such men as these.

These attributes not only apply to the lost, but to Christians who continue to be under the influence of the world. We must understand that scriptures were written to and for believers. Paul told Timothy to avoid these types of people for they would be present among the people of God.

Even today, we find individuals in the local church who exhibit many of these traits. We must pray for them and ourselves, that none of these traits would rule in our lives. We must strive to be different.

In order to overcome the world, we must

know what is in it. John gives us a three-dimensional description of what is in the world.

> *For all that is in the world, the lust of the flesh and the lust of the eyes and the boastful pride of life, is not from the Father; but is from the world. (I John 2:16)*

The three dimensions of the world are: 1) lust of the eyes, 2) lust of the flesh, and 3) pride of life. These are designed to keep us in bondage to sin. It, then, becomes our responsibility to separate ourselves from the world and the lusts that are present in it. It is only then that we will be able to gain victory over the flesh. Let us consider in greater depth the three dimensions of the world.

The story of David and Bathsheba gives a clear illustration of how the three aspects of the world can operate in the believer's life. As we consider this well-known account, we shall see how the lust of the eyes, the lust of the flesh, and the pride of life led to David's fall. The same would be true for the believer if there were no separation from worldly influences. In II Samuel 11, the account of David and Bathsheba is found. From the first verse, we can see what led to David's fall.

Then it happened in the spring, at the time when kings go out to the battle, that David sent Joab and his servants with him and all Israel, and they destroyed the sons of Ammon and besieged Rabbah. But David stayed at Jerusalem. (II Samuel 11:1)

At the time when battles were fought, King David remained home. He should have gone out to battle, because it was the time when "kings" went to fight. David remained home, neglecting his duties as king.

7

The lesson learned is that Christians cannot shun their responsibilities toward God. We must learn to remain faithful to reading and praying. Do not neglect to assemble together with other believers for mutual fellowship and encouragement. We should also strive to keep ourselves unspotted from the world's influences.

Pure religion and undefiled before God and the Father is this, to visit the fatherless and widows in their affliction, and to keep himself unspotted from the world. (James 1:27 KJV)

David's first mistake was that he got relaxed. Consequently, he found himself disconnected from Israel. The above verse states that "all Israel" went to fight. "All Israel" consisted of David's commanding officers, generals, as well as the soldiers. He had no accountability. His close servants were away. He had no one who could deter his behavior and correct him.

Anytime the believer discontinues fellowship with others, he will become a prey for the devil and the enticements of the world.

Not only must the believer attend church services regularly, but fellowship with other believers outside the church setting also. Some believers attend scheduled church services and they still fall into the allure of the world. Oftentimes, this occurs because there is no fellowship with believers on a consistent basis. If we are not careful, we will end up as David did; who consequently, became vulnerable to the first dimension of the world – the lust of the eyes.

Lust of the Eyes

The world has gained control over men and

women through one major force – the power of enticement (lust). Satan has designed the world and its system to be glamorous in the eyes of mankind. The eyes have been called the "gateway into the soul." Our eyes are avenues in which images enter into our being. Based on what we see, we make choices and take certain actions.

We must be careful about what we allow our eyes to behold, especially images that will lead us to lust. David would not have made the wrong choice, if he had not liked what he had seen. The beauty that he saw led to desire in his flesh. The "lust of the eyes" trapped him.

Now when evening came, David arose from his bed and walked around on the roof of the king's house, and from the roof he saw a woman bathing; and the woman was very beautiful to look upon. (II Samuel 11:2)

King David went out upon the roof and **saw** a woman, who was beautiful to **look** upon. Proverbs 27:20 says that the eyes of man are never satisfied. Because of his sinful nature, man's flesh will never be satisfied. He will always want more.

David, in a moment of weakness, became subject to what is written in Proverbs. His eyes were not satisfied; he saw and then lusted after Bathsheba. The lust of the eyes stirs up fleshly lusts, subsequently, leading to the fulfillment of those lusts.

Even today, the lust of the eyes control men and women. Usually, a husband or wife does not fall into adultery overnight. Oftentimes, it begins with him or her seeing someone who is physically attractive to them. Visual stimulation is the basis of pornography's control. Commercials on television are designed to entice. They make products pleasing to the sight; that their products may be purchased. Everything is based on sight and not reality. We usually eat at certain restaurants because of how the food looks. Individuals shop at a particular mall because it looks interesting.

The world is designed to tempt. If you have visited Las Vegas, you will find beautiful buildings; yet, many of these buildings are places that promote gambling and sexual immorality. The world makes everything look good: from immorality to substance abuse. If the believer is to be separate from the world, he must not be taken in by the lusts of the eyes. Though things may be appealing to the eyes, we must be on guard. The Bible tells us to avoid the very appearance of evil. Persons and objects that are not good for us will usually look good to us.

We must allow ourselves to be subject to the Spirit of God; that we will not be deceived. We must remember that the lust of the eyes stir up fleshly lusts; consequently, leading to the fulfillment of those lusts. David fell victim to this process. The lust of his eyes made him subject to the second dimension of the world – the lust of the flesh.

Lust of the Flesh

As the story of David and Bathsheba continues, we find that lust has enveloped David and he seeks information on Bathsheba. The lust of his eyes birthed lust in his flesh.

So, David sent and inquired about the woman. And one said, "Is not this Bathsheba, the daughter of Eliam, the wife of Uriah the Hittite?" (II Samuel 11:3)

King David sought this information with one goal, one purpose, and one desire. He wanted to fulfill those carnal urges that were present in his flesh. After he discovers who she is, he immediately sends for her. He then fulfills the lust in his flesh. Afterwards, he sends her away.

> *And David sent messengers and took her, and when she came to him, he lay with her; and when she had purified herself from her uncleanness, she returned to her home. (II Samuel 11:4)*

It is important to understand David's status as king. In this position, he could have had as many wives and concubines as he wanted. He could have almost any woman he wanted in the kingdom. David knew the commandments of God. He was not only a king, but also a prophet (Acts 2:29-30). Yet, in spite of this, lust controlled him.

David did not allow the Spirit of the Lord to govern him. Lust ruled and blinded David. When lust enters into the heart, sin is soon to follow (James 1:15). David was so blinded that after discovering Bathsheba was married, he still desired her and made steps towards having her.

As believers, we must not fall into this trap. The world is designed to create lust in our flesh. Not only does the world cause lust through visual enticement, but it also provides men and women with the resources to fulfill those lusts. There are many businesses, bars, restaurants, shops, and stores around the world with one mission – to fulfill the carnal desires of man. Believers are to walk circumspectly in the world.

Therefore, be careful how you walk, not as unwise men, but as wise. Make the most of your time because the days are evil. (Ephesians 5:15-16)

We are to live carefully and with wisdom. The

Christian must not be ignorant of his surroundings. As believers, we have to be honest about the areas in our lives that are sources of temptations. One major mistake of believers is that they deny, oftentimes, that they have weaknesses present in their flesh. We must be careful not to wear religious masks.

Recognizing areas of temptation will keep us aware of potential pitfalls when out in the world. The Christian must be discerning when he is out in the world. The believer is not to frequent every shop and business. These places are not evil, in and of themselves, but can provided sources of temptation that the believer must be aware of. The world not only encourages people to fulfill their lusts, but it provides the necessary means to do it.

As noted earlier, David sends Bathsheba home after they slept together. Not long after, Bathsheba sends word to David that she is pregnant (II Samuel 11:5). This was not how David thought things would turn out. David did not consider the consequences of his actions.

Believers must never be deceived in their thinking. Sin always has consequences. Remember that Paul exhorted the Galatians by telling them that they should not be deceived in their minds. He told them that whatever a man sows, he reaps. David did not think of this. Now, he has to find a way to cover up what he has done. He came up with an almost perfect plan to hide this unwanted pregnancy. David's scheme to cover up his sin was caused by pride. David wanted to keep his "righteous" image as king. His fleshly lust caused him to be vulnerable to the third dimension of the world – the pride of life.

Pride of Life

Pride has been the downfall of many men

and women in history. Proverbs tells us that pride comes before destruction (Proverbs 16:18). Pride was one of the major reasons why God destroyed Sodom and Gomorrah, not homosexuality.

> *Behold, this was the guilt of your sister Sodom: she and her daughters had arrogance (pride), abundant food, and careless ease, but she did not help the poor and needy. (Ezekiel 16:49 Parenthesis mine)*

In addition, pride was the reason God cast Lucifer and the angels that followed him out of heaven. Because of how God created him, he became arrogant and puffed up. His beauty and wisdom caused him to want to be God.

> *You had the seal of perfection, full of wisdom and perfect in beauty. You were blameless in your ways from the day you*

were created, until unrighteousness was found in you. But you said in your heart, "I will ascend to heaven, I will raise my thrown above the stars of God." Nevertheless, you will be thrust to Sheol, to the recesses of the pit. (Ezekiel 28:12, 15; Isaiah 14:13, 15)

Believers must avoid pride at all cost. Pride causes the judgment of God to be revealed. Pride also causes a separation from God. James 4:6 tells us that God resists those that are proud. Therefore, it is imperative that we humble ourselves before God, that He will bestow His grace upon us.

Pride manifests itself in various ways. We shall examine three aspects of the pride of life that can surface in the lives of believers. Each is deceptive and will cause the believer to become separated from God and captive to the enemy and his devices. The first aspect of the pride of life manifests itself when men and women practice sin, but cover it up that they may appear righteous before others. David fell into this form of pride.

Christians often fall into this trap whenever they try to justify their sin and declare their own righteousness because of their works. Through Christ alone, we gain true righteousness! For centuries, man has tried to appear just before God and one another, overlooking the fact that righteousness comes from God. Consequently, they miss the righteousness of God. Pride has blinded them as Paul describes,

> *For not knowing about God's righteousness, and seeking to establish their own righteousness, they did not subject themselves to the righteousness of God. (Romans 10:3)*

Within this scripture, we see that the pride

of life will cause believers to try in their own strength to be righteous. Righteousness is only obtained through faith and is not achieved through works. Righteous acts are an outward sign of inward faith. We must strive for the righteousness of God and not for the approval of others.

Continuing our examination of David and Bathsheba, we see what David did to preserve his righteous image after discovering Bathsheba's pregnancy.

And David sent to Joab, saying, Send me Uriah the Hittite. And Joab sent Uriah to David. And when Uriah was come unto him, David asked of him how Joab did, and how the people fared, and how the war prospered. And David said to Uriah, Go down to thy house, and wash thy feet. And Uriah departed out of the king's house, and there followed him a mess of food from the king. But Uriah slept at the door of the king's house with all the servants of his lord, and went not down to his house. And when they had told David, saying, Uriah went not down unto his house, David said unto Uriah, Art thou not come from a journey? Wherefore didst thou not go down unto thy house? And Uriah said unto David, The ark, and Israel, and Judah, abide in booths; and my lord Joab, and the servants of my lord, are encamped in the open field; shall I then go into my house, to eat and to drink, and to lie with my wife? as thou livest, and as thy soul liveth, I will not do this thing. And David said to Uriah, Tarry here to-day also, and to-morrow I will let thee depart. So Uriah abode in Jerusalem that day, and the morrow. And when David had called him, he did eat and drink before him; and he made him drunk: and at even he went out to lie on his bed with the servants of his lord, but went not down to his house. And it came to pass in the morning, that David wrote a letter to Joab, and sent it by the hand of Uriah. And he wrote in the letter, saying, Set ye Uriah in the forefront of the hottest battle, and retire ye from him, that he may be smitten, and die. (II Samuel 11:6-15)

Pride is a deceiver and will cause people to do almost anything, even kill, if it means preserving their image before others. The above verses show us that the pride of life can lead to numerous other sins. David abused his authority. He tried to deceive Uriah. And when this did not work, he finally conspires to have him killed. All of this occurred because of pride.

Even today, believers must be on guard against this. Oftentimes, we try to look "right" before one another. In trying to do so, we get involved in other things. Many times, believers will lie and put up facades to appear righteous. At the root of it all, the pride of life is present.

The second aspect of the pride of life manifests when individuals practice sin and lead lives that project that a sinful lifestyle is acceptable. They know the truth concerning God's standards, but choose to do otherwise. In this instance, the lifestyle demonstrated by believers who have a clear understanding of the commands of God as outlined in scripture. Paul addressed this mentality in his writings.

And, although they know the ordinance of God, that those who practice such things are worthy of death, they not only do the same, but also give a hearty approval to those who practice them. (Romans 1:32)

This form of pride will cause people, even

believers, to boast in their sin and encourage others to do the same. We have all encountered individuals that say, even though they smoke, drink, lie, and commit sexual immorality, they are still right with God. On the other hand, we have met individuals who tell us that it is O.K. to sin because we are only human and God understands.

This is deceptive and dangerous. It will cause men and women to continue in sin without fear. They do no not think God will judge them because nothing "bad" has happened to them in the past. They are deceived into thinking that it is proper for them to practice sin. However, Jeremiah 5:7-9 says,

Why should I pardon you? Your sons have forsaken me, and sworn by those who are not gods. When I had fed them to the full, they committed adultery and trooped to the harlot's house. They were well fed horses,

each one neighing for his neighbor's wife. Shall I not punish these people, declares the Lord?

If we look at the Israelites, it is clear that they fell into this form of the pride of life. In spite of God's blessings and commandments, they continued to sin. They continued to worship Baal and Ashtaroth. They even sacrificed to other gods in the temple. Because of their sinful nature, they offered up their children as sacrifices to pagan gods. Their lives imitated the sinful ways of the heathen nations surrounding them.

A hot iron seared their conscious (I Timothy 4:2). They believed that God was with them, in spite of their continual sin, and that no harm would befall them. As believers, we must avoid this form of pride at all costs. We must not fall into deception, believing that God will wink at or pass over our sins because we are Christians.

Paul asked the Romans, "Shall we continue in sin?" The answer is No! Although God offers forgiveness through Jesus, it is not an excuse to practice sin. It is written, "Where sin increased, grace abounded the much more (Galatians 5:20)." Grace is given to keep the judgment of God from us while we are resisting sin. Therefore, this scripture tells us that God has already supplied the grace and allotted time needed to overcome areas of weakness.

If the believer continues, practices, and lives in sin willfully, the grace of God may be withdrawn and His judgment displayed. This is what happened to Israel. God removed His mercy and caused them to go into Babylonian captivity. It is then imperative to recognize that even as the Israelites reaped destruction because of their sins, so shall it be for anyone who continues practicing sin without exercising repentance.

The third and most common form of the pride of life occurs when people become puffed up within themselves. They act as though everyone and everything is beneath them. They feel that they are exempt from certain things, though others may be subject to them. Looking once again at Bathsheba and David's story, we find that pride was the catalyst for all of the events that followed.

David became so confident in God and in his status as king, he did not go to war. He had become comfortable and remained in Jerusalem. He sent his commanding officers and soldiers into battle without him. When he remained home, he saw Bathsheba from his roof. All of this led to his downfall and God's judgment.

Believers must continue to humble themselves before God, commit to prayer and fasting, studying the Word, and attending services and fellowshipping with other believers. These things will keep our minds elevated and keep us from becoming carnal Christians.

As we have seen, David became subject to three dimensions of the world – the lust of the eyes, the lust of the flesh, and the pride of life. His story should serve as a warning and example to us all, if we are to live in victory in this world. We must remember that one lust will lead to another. If we can overcome these areas, we will be on the road to overcoming the world.

Defilement of Spirit

To conclude our examination of the world and its attributes, it is important that believers become aware of an area that must be guarded from the allure of the world.

The three aspects of the world (lust of the eyes, lust of the flesh, and the pride of life) deal primarily with desires birthed in the flesh. However, if we keep the world's pattern of thinking, we will fall into the aforementioned areas.

The believer must stay cautious at all times. He must allow his thought process to be governed by the Holy Spirit and the Word of God. The world is not only designed to keep our flesh in bondage, but also our minds and spirits. Paul lets us know that we must not only keep our flesh (bodies) clean, but also our spirits,

> ***Therefore having these promises, beloved, let us cleanse ourselves from all defilement of flesh and spirit, perfecting holiness in the fear of God. (II Corinthians 7:1)***

Paul is not saying the Holy Spirit in us needs to be cleansed, but our own human spirit. The human spirit is where thoughts, emotions, personality traits, and attributes come from.

God has given us many promises. Because Jesus overcame the world, the believer can also (John 16:33). He promised us power over the enemy, victory instead of defeat. Yet, the above scripture lets us know that to obtain these promises, we must cleanse ourselves. We are to cleanse our flesh and spirit. The flesh is to be cleansed since it is where sins are committed in the physical body. The spirit needs to be cleansed because it is where sins of the mind take place.

Some believers become deceived in their thinking in this area. They may feel that as long as they do not fornicate, commit adultery, smoke, or drink, then they are righteous. So, they neglect to correct the error that is in their spirit.

We should take into consideration that sin includes backbiting, lying, jealousy, envy, strife, stubbornness, rebellion, hatred, and the like. We have to allow the mind of Christ to be formed in us. The world not only dictates how to live, but it dictates how to behave also. The believer has to keep his spirit from being defiled. It is only then that we can be separate from the world.

Believers fail to cleanse their spirit from the world's influence because it is unseen. They are focused on keeping their physical activities pure while neglecting their mental activities. For they feel that as long as there is no outward sin, there is nothing to be concerned about.

Let us recall one of Jesus' teachings. He said that God was not only concerned with the acts of man, but more importantly with the heart of man. He stated that sinful acts were a direct result of what was in a person's spirit. Jesus taught His disciples saying,

For from within, out of the hearts of men, proceed the evil thoughts, fornications, thefts, murders, adulteries, deeds of coveting and wickedness, as well as deceit, sensuality, envy, slander, pride and foolishness. All these evil things proceed from within and defile the man. (Mark 7:21-23)

Jesus is teaching us that even our sinful acts are the result of what is in our spirits. It behooves us to cleanse our spirits because it can lead to sinful acts. Jesus rebuked the Pharisees because they thought the works of the law made them righteous. They had forgotten the spiritual aspects of the law.

On one occasion, the Pharisees had accused Jesus of breaking the law because He and His disciples plucked ears of corn and ate on the Sabbath. It was apparent that they were only concerned with the outward actions (Matthew 12:1-2). Therefore, He had to remind them that sin and error was not only in what a person did, but also in how they thought. He answered them by saying,

> *If you had known what these words mean, I desire mercy, not sacrifice; you would not have condemned the innocent. (Matthew 12:7 NIV)*

Jesus told them that God was more concerned with the spirit of the law (mercy) more than the works of law (sacrifice). We must also avoid falling into the same snare as the Pharisees. We should not only have righteous acts, but righteous hearts.

Earlier, we noted that Paul commanded those of Corinth to cleanse themselves from all defilement. If we look again closely at Paul's exhortation, we are told that two major areas to clean are the flesh and the spirit. Though everyone struggles with both of these areas, it is evident that some struggle in one area more than the other does.

Therefore, we can divide the church into these two groups. The first are those that struggle primarily in the flesh, and second are those who have problems in their spirit. Again, when we refer to the spirit, it is where the thought process, will, personality traits, and attitudes of the heart are resident.

In the popular parable of the Prodigal Son, we see these two groups portrayed in detail. The prodigal son represents those believers bound by worldly or fleshly desires. The older brother that remained home represents those believers who have to correct the error in their spirits.

And he said, A certain man had two sons: and the younger of them said to his father, Father, give me the portion of thy substance that falleth to me. And he divided unto them his living. And not many days after, the younger son gathered all together and took his journey into a far country; and there he wasted his substance with riotous living. (Luke 15:11-13)

In this story, it is easy to see the younger brother's error. His sins were external and open to the sight of others. It is apparent that he had a problem with his flesh. He wasted his money with loose living

And when he had spent all, there arose a mighty famine in that country; and he began to be in want. (Luke 15:14)

He spent all of his money on worldly pleasures.

The story does not indicate what this consisted of; however, it is clear that his main objective was to fulfill the desires of his flesh.

And he went and joined himself to one of the citizens of that country; and he sent him into his field to feed swine. And he would fain have filled his belly with the husks that the swine did eat: and no man gave unto him. But when he came to himself he said, How many hired servants of my father's have bread enough and to spare, and I perished here with hunger! I will arise and go to my father, and will say unto him, Father, I have sinned against heaven, and in thy sight: I am no more worthy to be called your son: make me as one of thy hired servants. And he arose, and came to his father. But while he was yet afar off, his father saw him, and was moved with compassion, and ran, and fell on his neck and kissed him. And the son said unto him, Father, I have sinned against heaven, and in thy sight: I am no more worthy to be called thy son. (Luke 15:15-21)

Though he had a problem with his flesh, he keeps his spirit clean. His reaction to his circumstances demonstrates this. After all had been taken away from him, he did not try to cover up his sin. He did not ever state that he was right in what he did. Instead, he acknowledges his error. He acknowledges it first within himself (verse 18), then to his father (verse 20). He recognizes his error, repents, and returns home.

Now his elder son was in the field: and as he came and drew nigh to the house, he heard music and dancing. And he called to him one of the servants, and inquired what these things might be. And he said unto him, Thy brother is come; and thy father hath killed the fatted calf, because he hath received him safe and sound. But he was angry, and would not go in: and his father came out, and entreated him. (Luke 15:25-28)

We do not recognize the error in the older brother until the latter part of the parable. When his brother returned home, jealousy, and envy surfaced in him. He would not talk to his father or his brother. At first, he appears as any good son. He had remained home and served his father. We, then, discover that his spirit was defiled. His anger and frustration began to surface.

But he answered and said to his father, Lo, these many years do I serve thee, and I never transgressed a commandment of thine; and yet thou never gavest me a kid, that I might make merry with my friends:

but when this thy son came, who hath devoured thy living with harlots, thou killedst for him the fatted calf. (Luke 15:29-30)

A root of bitterness sprang up in the older brother (Hebrews 12:15). He did not attend the celebration for his returned brother. He did not want to be a part of it. The brother was caught in the world's way of thinking. He thought that he was better than his younger brother. In addition, he felt that he deserved the party rather than his brother. Because his spirit was defiled, he fell into the three dimensions of the world.

First, the lusts of the eyes overtook him when he saw what was done for his brother and he became jealous. Second, the lust of the flesh subdued him when he desired to have what his brother had. Finally, the pride of life surfaced when he made every effort possible to show his father how good and deserving he was. He thought the father should remember how faithful he had been and remember his works. He also tries to show his father how undeserving his brother was. In the end, his father reproved him for his thinking.

And he said unto him, Son, thou art ever with me, and all that is mine is thine. But it was meet to take merry and be glad: for this thy brother was dead, and is alive again; and was lost, and is found. (Luke 15:31-32)

The world is designed to flow totally opposite to the Church's teachings. The world teaches that you must love those that love you (Luke 6:32) and hate those that hate you. Jesus taught that we must love those that intentionally use us.

The world tells you to go with what you feel and say what is on your mind. On the other hand, we are taught of God to "be angry and sin not." The world says be proud of who you are. It tells you to render evil for evil and to live for yourself. Conversely, we are taught in the Word to only boast in God and do good unto all men, even our enemies.

It is obvious that if any believer adopts the world's way of thinking, his spirit will be defiled. Even Jesus had to correct the disciples for operating in the wrong frame of thought. When they were rejected in a certain city, they asked Jesus if they should call fire down from heaven. Jesus told them that they did not know what kind of spirit they were operating in (Luke 9:55). It is imperative that we strive to maintain a clean spirit, or we will fall into this same trap.

Since a defiled spirit is not physically seen, believers operate in error without being corrected. Oftentimes, believers who have a defilement of spirit will criticize those who have a defilement of the flesh. This is because the other's sin is readily seen.

When considering the parable of the Prodigal Son, we find this to be true. The brother who had a defiled spirit accused him that had the defilement of the flesh to their father.

In another of Jesus' parables, we find another example of this scenario in action. Jesus spoke a parable contrasting the difference in how a Pharisee prayed and how a tax collector prayed. The Pharisee, during his prayer, boasted about his righteous acts and criticized the tax collector whose acts were not so wonderful.

The Pharisee stood and was praying thus to himself, "God, I thank thee that I am not like other people: swindlers, unjust, adulterers, or even like this tax-gatherer. I

fast twice a week; I pay tithes of all I get."
(Luke 18:11-12)

The Pharisee had a defiled spirit. His life included righteous acts, but his heart was puffed up. Because his sin was not "open" for all to view, he thought himself better than the tax collector and verbally bragged about it in his prayer. How different people can be when dealing with sin! For we find in the same parable that the tax collector prayed also. Though his flesh was defiled, we find that his heart was right. He acknowledged his sin,

But the tax-gatherer, standing some distance away, was even unwilling to lift up his eyes to heaven, but was beating his breast, saying, "God be merciful to me, a sinner!" (Luke 18:13)

The tax collector kept a humble spirit before

God. Yet, we see the dynamics of this parable demonstrated in the Church today. When someone is found in an open sin, others circle around him or her and say, "I thank God it was not for me!" Instead of trying to restore them (Galatians 6:1), they condemn them. However, we see at the end of the parable who was right with God.

> *I will tell you, this man (the tax-gatherer) went down to his house justified rather than the other; for every one that exalts himself shall be humbled, but he who humbles himself shall be exalted. (Luke 18:14 Parentheses mine)*

Jesus' words should serve as a warning to all that will condemn others. Only God knows the heart. The tax collector, who had unrighteous acts, left from prayer justified by God rather than the Pharisee. We must remember the words that Jesus spoke,

Do not judge lest you be judged. For in the way you judge, you will be judged; and by your standard of measure, it will be measure unto you. (Matthew 7:1-2)

God judged the Pharisee because he had judged the tax collector. He went home unjustified in the eyesight of God. This should challenge us to keep our spirits clean; that we may be found blameless before God. We must ask God continually to help us recognize error in our spirit. If we do this, we can overcome all that the world presents to us.

We must remember that to overcome the world, we first have to separate ourselves from the world, including certain individuals. The believer must be on guard at all times in order to avoid the deception of the world's glamour (lust of the eyes), to shun what the world has to offer (lust of the flesh), to not use the world's standard of righteousness (pride of life).

Once we have taken steps towards separating ourselves from these things, God can cleanse our hearts and minds. Our spirits can be renewed in righteousness. We will then be true sons and daughters of God, as He intended for us to be. God wants us to separate from the world and its things.

Do not be bound together with unbelievers; for what partnership has righteousness with lawlessness, or what fellowship has light with darkness? Or what harmony hath Christ with Belial, or what has a believer in common with an unbeliever? Or what agreement has the temple of God with idols? For we are the temples of the living God; just as God said, "I will dwell in them and walk among them; and I will be their God, and they shall be My people. Therefore come out from their midst and be separate," says the Lord. "And do not touch what is unclean; and I will welcome you. And I will be a father to you, and you shall be sons and daughters to Me," says the Lord Almighty. (II Corinthians 6:14-18)

It is through separation from the world, that we can fully become sons and daughters of God. Moreover, once this is achieved, we can overcome the world. Yet, after we fully separate ourselves from the world, we must not stop. We must then conquer the next battleground – the flesh.

Section 2

▼

The Flesh

For I know that nothing good dwells in me, that is, in my flesh. – Romans 7:18

Mankind has been under the control of sin since his early existence. Sin dwells in the flesh of man. Paul knew that the temptation to sin did not cease after being converted; therefore, he taught that our spirit is the only thing that can be renewed and not the flesh. How true!

The flesh cannot be renewed and nothing good can abide in it. Thus, to conquer the flesh, it has to be brought under the authority of Christ. I Corinthians 9:26 states that Paul had to discipline his body (flesh) and bring it under control.

We can only bring the flesh under control when we walk in honesty. Though we are believers, we must not deceive ourselves.

> *The heart is deceitful above all things, and it is exceedingly perverse and corrupt and severely, mortally sick! Who can know it [perceive, understand, and be acquainted with his own heart and mind]? (Jeremiah 17:9 Amplified)*

The scriptures warn us to guard our hearts and minds. Why? Our hearts and minds can deceive us. We must make sure we know what is in them. We must acknowledge our capacity to sin.

> *If we say we have no sin, we are deceiving ourselves, and the truth is not in us. If we confess our sins, He is faithful and just to forgive our sins and to cleanse us from all unrighteousness. (I John 1:8-9)*

The Holy Spirit in us causes us to face the sinful nature. If He is in us, we will see our true state. It is only in acknowledging our sins can we receive forgiveness and cleansing.

Because it is our desire to be just before God, oftentimes, we will not want to let Him see those things in us that are not so good. It becomes difficult to confess our sins when we fall more than once. However, we must be open with Him in order to overcome the flesh.

Every believer faces temptation daily. To overcome it, we must realize where the source of temptation comes from. The scriptures clearly teach that God does not cause the temptation to sin. It appears that this fact is accepted unquestionably. Yet consistently, when a believer falls into temptation and sins, he sometimes will exclaim, "The devil made me do it!" Men and women have used this excuse for centuries. From the very beginning, it was used. The Book of Genesis records that Eve used this excuse. God confronted Adam and Eve after they had eaten the forbidden fruit. God asked her why she did it, and she blamed the devil,

Then the Lord God said to the woman, "What is this you have done?" And the woman (Eve) said, "The serpent deceived me, and I ate. (Genesis 3:13 Parentheses mine)

James commands his readers not to blame God when they are tempted to sin. We must remember not to blame the devil either,

Let no one say when he is tempted, "I am being tempted by God;" for God cannot be tempted by evil, and He himself does not tempt anyone. But each one is tempted when he is carried away and enticed by his

own lust. *(James 1:13-14)*

James explains why one is tempted. Temptation comes as a result of the lust that is already resident in the flesh. We all have been born with the capacity to sin. The Bible identifies Adam as the father of man. When he sinned, we all sinned with him. Therefore, everyone born after him comes forth in sin (Romans 5:12).

Since the fall of Adam and Eve, man has always struggled with the inborn trait of sin. David exclaimed that he was brought forth in iniquity (Psalms 51:5). Even Paul, in his frustration told of his struggle with the flesh calling himself a wretched man (Romans 7:24). We must remember this when we are tempted to sin. If it is a temptation to us, then that lust is in our flesh.

With the discovery of the existence of

demons and the reality of spiritual warfare, believers today continue to place the blame for their desire to sin on the devil. Believers have become so "spirit-conscience" that they fail to realize that what they are calling a spirit is actually a characteristic of the flesh.

Because of this, believers fail to crucify the flesh and mortify its deeds. If someone is upset, it is said, "He has a spirit of anger." If someone is full of pride, it is said, "He has a spirit of pride." In addition, if someone operates in lust, it is said, "He has a spirit of lust." Yet, the scriptures call all of these characteristics deeds of the flesh.

Therefore, when sinful desires manifest in the flesh, the believer does not deal with his flesh, but rather places the blame on a "spirit." The believer is deceived. He will inevitably lead a defeated life because he will feel something beyond his control causes his sinful desires. He is, in actuality, fighting with an imaginary enemy. Paul tells us:

I therefore so run, not as uncertainly; so fight I, not as one that beateth the air. (I Corinthians 9:26)

When the believer cannot discern between what is flesh and what is a demonic spirit, he is running uncertainly and fighting as one beating the air. It is important to note that before one can deal with the flesh, he must first be able to discern what is his flesh and what is a spirit.

Distinguishing between flesh and spirit is simpler than what believers have been traditionally taught. Believers have exposed to numerous teachings concerning the spiritual realm and demons. Many have taught that Christians cannot have demons, while others believe that it is possible. They have been taught that demons are not real and that they are real. The list goes on and on.

In spite of all of these teachings, believers continue to struggle in their flesh on a daily basis. To simplify the subject of what is flesh and what is spirit, one must only look to the Word. Jesus also addressed the subject by saying:

When the unclean spirit is gone out of a man, he walketh through dry places, seeking rest; and finding none, he saith, I will return unto my house whence I came out. And when he cometh, he findeth it swept and garnished. Then goeth he, and taketh to him seven other spirits more wicked than himself; and they enter in, and dwell there: and the last state of that man is worse than the first. (Luke 11:24-26)

Jesus says that once an unclean spirit leaves out of

a man, it looks for a place to rest. If it cannot find a new home, it will return to the man it came out of. Once back, it finds the man (house) is empty and clean. We must be wise. If we do not fill our "house" with Christ and the Word after we are delivered from bondage, the enemy may be able to put us back into bondage. The enemy has no more control over a believer than what the believer gives him.

When an individual is converted, the power and control of sin is broken in his life. Still, many new converts are neither strong nor knowledgeable enough to maintain freedom in every area of their lives. Does this mean that spirits will be in them? Of course not!

The principle set forth in this scripture is that a spirit *may* be present when there is an area of weakness in the flesh, which is not submitted to Christ.

Therefore, distinguishing between what is flesh and spirit is simple. Again, wherever there is a weakness, the potential for a spirit to operate there is present. We must realize also that once the weak area is overcome, the door to the enemy is closed. We must learn to close every door to the enemy. If we deal with our sinful desires, the concern with spirits will decrease and we can focus wholly on our personal walk with God. The goal is not to necessarily fight the enemy or temptation, but to draw closer to God.

How then do we draw closer to God and overcome the flesh? We face temptation daily. We not only have to deal with outside influences, but with our own internal desires. We shall now look at steps to overcome the flesh. These steps are not the rule, but they provide general guidelines that we can follow to victory.

In the first section, we discussed the world and its

attributes. Again, we must understand that the flesh cannot be overcome until all ties with the world are severed. Overcoming the world and its influences is the first step to overcoming the flesh.

Remember that in order to overcome the world, we must not only avoid physical temptation, but also avoid thinking as the world does. Once this is achieved, you will be in a position, as stated earlier, to deal with the flesh without any outside influence.

Denial of the Flesh

The second step to overcoming the flesh is to practice self-control. Do not give your flesh everything that it craves. More importantly, do not give your flesh its sinful desires.

And He was saying unto them all, "If anyone wishes to come after me, let him deny himself, and take up his cross daily, and follow me." (Luke 9:23)

Jesus said that in order to follow Him, we must deny ourselves. He commands us to give up those selfish and fleshly desires. Only then will we be able to live as He has destined for us to live. To gain control over the flesh, the believer must be consistent in denying it.

The flesh can be compared to a snake. One of the unique abilities of a snake is that it does not eat on a regular basis. A snake is able to eat and feed on it from 1 day up to 3 weeks, depending on the size of the meal. When a believer succumbs to the desires of the flesh, it is like giving it a feeding.

Oftentimes, after we have sinned, we will feel remorse and no longer have a desire to sin in that area again. It is during this time that we often think that we are delivered and have overcome, because the desire is not present. A snake has to eat again after a span of time.

Likewise, the desires of the flesh will want to be fulfilled again. This is where many believers become discouraged and give up. Because when they thought they were delivered, the desire returned. They never realized that they were never fully delivered.

We must realize that because the desire for a particular sin is not always on our minds, it does not mean that we are delivered. Only denying sinful desires consistently will give us the victory. After Jesus was tested by the devil, it is recorded that the devil left him for a season (Luke 4:13 KJV). He only left Jesus alone for a time, and he would return. Our desires operate in the same way, even when we deny them.

Because we have one victory, the struggles

will not end. Every time the desire for sin comes, we must resist it or we will live in defeat. Jesus defeated the enemy during His tests, but the enemy would come again. We must not become discouraged when the desires return. It does not mean we are not free. In order to remain free, we must consistently deny the impulses. Even though we are instructed to deny the flesh, some are still unclear as to how to do it. One way to deny the flesh is to submit to God.

Submit to God. Resist the devil and he will flee from you. (James 4:7)

We can only resist evil temptations after we submit to God. Sometimes, we try to overcome without God's help. When yielded to God, nothing will be impossible. The way we submit to God is to obey the Word and follow the leading of the Holy Spirit. As we do these things, we will deny the flesh and bring it under control.

Consecration through Prayer and Fasting

The third step to overcoming the flesh is to consecrate our bodies unto God through prayer and fasting.

I urge you therefore, brethren, by the mercies of God, to present your bodies a living and holy sacrifice, acceptable to God, which is your spiritual service of worship. And do not be conformed to this world, but be ye transformed by the renewing of your mind, that you many prove what the will of God is, that which is good and acceptable and perfect. (Romans 12:1-2)

Believers must present their bodies unto God as if they are offering up a sacrifice unto him. Under the Old Covenant, the Jews had to come before God with sacrifices and burnt offerings for forgiveness of sin. The sacrifices during this time were only a shadow of the sacrifice that Christ would ultimately make on Calvary. He was the perfect sacrifice for sin.

With Jesus being the ultimate sacrifice, sacrifices under the Levitical system were rendered null and void. God now requires a living sacrifice, not a dead one. He no longer wants animals, but asks that we give Him our very bodies. Our total being is to be given to God – mind, body, and soul. By giving ourselves to Him, we give Him full control of our lives. This is further illustrated in Hebrews 10:4-6,

For it is impossible for the blood of bulls and goats to take away sins. Therefore, when he comes into the world, he says, "Sacrifice and burnt offerings thou hast not desired, but a body thou hast prepared for me; in whole burnt offerings and sacrifices for sin, thou hast taken no

pleasure. "

God sent Jesus into the world to be the perfect
sacrifice. God no longer wanted animals, so
He prepared Jesus a human body to bring Him
into the world. It was in this body that He made
the ultimate sacrifice. He is our example. As
He offered up His body unto God, we must also.
God desires a sacrifice that will bring Him honor
and glory. The believer must fast and pray to
present his body to God. It is the only way the
body can be presented to Him, holy and
acceptable.

Prayer combined with fasting is the key to
consecration. Without prayer and fasting, we will
have some dominion over the flesh, but will never
rule it. We must possess both of these disciplines.
Prayer is not as effective as it can be without
fasting; likewise, fasting is ineffectual without
prayer.

In Philippians 3:19, Paul speaks of individuals "whose God is their stomach." This signifies that their fleshly appetites ruled them. Without the discipline of fasting, the belly (fleshly appetites) will become god in the life of the believer. Fasting is essential, though many devalue its use. There are certain scholars who affirm that fasting is just another aspect of the law and should not be practiced by believers. Jesus, himself, affirmed that we would fast,

> *And John's disciples and the Pharisees were fasting; and they came and said to him, "Why do John's disciples and the disciples of the Pharisees fast, but your disciples do not fast?" And Jesus said to them, "While the bridegroom is with them, the attendants of the bridegroom do not fast, do they? So long as they have the bridegroom with them, they cannot fast. But the days will come when the*

bridegroom is taken away from them, and then they will fast in that day. (Mark 9:28-29)

Aside from some teaching that we should not fast because it is an Old Testament practice, others do not see how it can aid in their walk with God. Some even ask, "How can my abstaining from food help discipline my flesh when I have other desires besides eating?" The answer is not a difficult one. The stomach is called the center of the human body. In examining this statement, the answer to our question is easily discovered.

When looking at the stomach and its role in the human body, it is easy to understand why it is called the center of the body. When the body needs nutrients, hunger comes into the stomach. Various sicknesses originate in the stomach. Oftentimes, when one becomes extremely angry, it starts with a hot and sometimes ill feeling in the stomach. The stomach experiences nausea and queasiness when one is troubled or afraid. Even when the urge for sexual gratification arises, it is often felt first in the stomach.

If the stomach is connected to all of these things, then it is true that fasting can tame other fleshly desires. The stomach is an area where many fleshly desires originate. Fasting not only brings the appetite for food under control, but also fleshly desires. Remember though, fasting is most effective when combined with prayer. When the disciples could not cast the devil out of the boy who had a deaf and dumb spirit, they questioned Jesus as to why the boy was not delivered,

And when he was come into the house, his disciples asked him privately, "Why could we not cast him out?" And he aid unto

them, "This kind cometh forth by nothing, but prayer and fasting." (Mark 9:28-29)

Jesus' answer gives insight into why some vulnerable areas remain in the believer's life. Until the flesh is put into subjection by prayer *and* fasting, the enemy will always have influence in our lives. Jesus told them that this particular spirit is not removed except through prayer and fasting. If certain spirits are not expelled except through prayer and fasting together, then it is understood that certain areas in our flesh cannot be overcome but by the same means.

If we do not follow this, we will become frustrated and embarrassed in our walk with God, as the disciples were frustrated and embarrassed because they could not cast out the spirit. Many believers have become frustrated because they continue to fail in the war against their flesh. This is because they will not take out

69

the time to discipline the body through prayer and fasting. Many are looking for an instantaneous victory.

There are no shortcuts to victory over the flesh. Consider the disciples. Jesus gave them authority to cast out spirits in His name; yet, they could not cast out this particular spirit. Though they had the authority, they would have to add prayer and fasting to that authority. It is the same with us. We must add prayer and fasting to the authority that God has given us.

Prayer is most essential because it helps our spirit to be in tune with the Holy Spirit. Payer helps the believer to be conscious of God's indwelling presence. It helps the believer to yield to the Holy Spirit. When we yield to the Spirit, we will exercise dominion over the flesh. If we do not yield, the flesh will rule, for it fights against the Spirit.

But I say, walk by the Spirit, and you will not carry our the desire of the flesh. For the flesh sets its desires against the Spirit, and the Spirit against the flesh; for these are in opposition to one another, so that you may not to do the things that you please. (Galatians 5:16-17)

Since the Spirit and the flesh war against one another, it is important for us to be in the Spirit. Prayer causes us to recognize the voice of the Spirit and follow His instructions. In addition, prayer helps the believer to be aware of the devil's tactics. Prayer connects us with God and helps us to know His will for our lives. Prayer is further strengthened when we use the scriptures in our prayers.

We, oftentimes, look for some formula when it comes to prayer. The only thing that we need to remember in prayer is to use the Word. God's

Word is established forever. Using the Word in prayer causes the promises of God to manifest in your life, even in warfare against the flesh. The Word causes prayer to be powerful and effective. On the other hand, prayer is not as effective as it can be when there is no discipline in the life of the believer. Fasting is where discipline comes from. Therefore, it is understood that to walk in total victory over the flesh, we need fasting along with prayer.

Walk in Forgiveness

The fourth step to overcoming the flesh is to walk in forgiveness. Jesus died for the sins of the world. He died once, for all of our sins: past, present, and future. Once we are converted, we can believe that God has forgiven us for all of our past sins. When we sin after conversion, we think that God will not forgive us now because we really did not know and love Him as we should. How untrue!

It is this thinking that keeps some believers in bondage. They feel that God will not forgive them, so they do not forgive themselves. They stop trying to overcome the flesh. Guilt and shame overcomes them. Remember, God's provision for sin stands even after we are converted.

My little children, I am writing these things to you that you may not sin. And if anyone sins, we have an advocate with the Father, Jesus Christ the righteous; and He himself is the propitiation for our sins; and not for ours only, but also for the whole world. (I John 2:1-2)

John wrote to believers to keep them from sinning. However, he states that if they did sin, they had an advocate or lawyer before God. He lets us know that even if we sin presently, Jesus will make intercession to the Father for our forgiveness. After understanding all of these things, some do not think that it can be that simple. However, the scriptures say,

Come now, and let us reason together, says the Lord. Though your sins are as scarlet, they will be white as snow; though they are red like crimson, they shall be like wool. (Isaiah 1:18)

If we have sinned, God wants us to come to Him. He wants to help and forgive us so that He can wash us. Proverbs tells us that we should acknowledge God in all of our ways. We fail to realize this refers also to our sinful ways. For in doing so, God can direct us as to how to overcome. Isaiah prophetically reveals to us the heart of God. He wants us to come to Him as a Father and He wants to not only forgive us, but cleanse us also.

Who is a God like Thee, who pardons iniquity and passes over the rebellious acts

of the remnant of His possession? He does not retain His anger forever because He delights in unchanging love. He will again have compassion on us. He will tread our iniquities under foot. Yes, Thou wilt cast all their sins into the depths of the sea. (Micah 7:18-19)

Micah tells us that God pardons iniquities and passes over rebellious acts. A rebellious act is an action that is done intentionally. God will forgive us and cast our sins into the depths of the sea. Our sins will become "lost at sea." God offers forgiveness. Not only will He forgive, but He will also forget.

I, even I, and the one who wipes out your transgressions for my own sake and I will not remember your sins. Put me in remembrance, let us argue our case together, and state your cause that you may be proved right. (Isaiah 43:25)

We must understand that God loved us so much that He ultimately sent His only Son to die. Why did He die? He died so that we could receive *forgiveness* for our sins. If we would only accept the forgiveness that God has provided for us through Christ. We would be able to move in faith knowing that He will help us in our fight to overcome the flesh. He provides forgiveness to shield us from His judgment until we are delivered.

Patience

The final step to overcoming the flesh is to exercise patience. When we have struggles in the flesh, we want an instantaneous deliverance. We want to pray once and receive the "touch" from the Spirit of God and be free. We must give ourselves time to walk in deliverance. The Word tells us that it is through patience that we inherit the promises of God. One of His promises is that we will no longer live under the bondage of sin.

> *Cast not away therefore your confidence, which has great recompense of reward. For ye have need of patience, that after you have done the will of God, ye might receive the promise. (Hebrews 10:35-36)*

In our efforts to overcome the flesh, we must always believe that we can be delivered. If we retain our faith, we will receive a great reward. The reward will be victory over sin while we are yet in these mortal bodies. We must have patience. We need patience after we have done the will of God.

After we have prayed, fasted, and studied the Word, we must then exercise patience until we see the fruit of our labor in overcoming the desires of the flesh. Paul told the Galatians they ought not to be deceived, for whatever a man sows that is what he is going to reap. If we sow to our spiritual lives, we will reap righteousness and victory over the flesh.

The enemy comes as a deceiver and tells us, "You have prayed, fasted, and asked God to help you. Then, why are you not yet delivered? You should give up because there is no hope for you." We must recognize his lies and remember this exhortation of scripture,

> *God forbid: yea, let God be true, but every man a liar; as it is written, that thou mayest be justified in thy sayings, and mightest overcome when thou art judged. (Romans 3:4 KJV)*

We must allow the truth of the Word to remain in

our minds and the patience of God to rule our hearts until we gain control over the flesh. If we will do this, our struggles with the flesh will turn into victories.

The steps needed to overcome the flesh should now be settled in your mind. The first step is to separate yourself from the world and its influence in your life. The second step is to deny the sinful desires of the flesh consistently. Third, consecrate your body to God through prayer and fasting.

Next, you are to walk in the forgiveness that God has provided. Finally, exercise patience until victory is achieved. If these steps are not taken, the believer will not overcome his flesh and have the power to face the enemy. We have authority over the enemy, but we must do our part.

Behold, I have given you authority to tread

upon serpents and scorpions, and over all the power of the enemy, and nothing shall injure you. (Luke 10:19)

If we will not separate from the world and crucify the flesh, we will be defeated instead of victorious. The believer will be no match for the enemy, even though in Christ, we have dominion over him.

And if I by Beelzebub cast out demons, by whom do your sons cast them out? Consequently, they shall be your judges. But if I cast out demons by the Spirit of God, then the kingdom of God is upon you. Or how can anyone enter the strong man's house and carry out his property, unless he first binds the strong man? And then he will plunder his house. (Matthew 12:27-29)

Jesus exercised power and authority against

the enemy. As his followers, we can also. In the aforementioned verses, Jesus informs us that unless the enemy (strong man) is bound, he cannot be defeated. When the believer separates from the world and overcomes his flesh, the enemy is prohibited from operating in his life.

In the introduction, we looked at how Jesus defeated the enemy. However, he did not defeat him until he separated himself from the world and overcame His flesh though prayer and fasting. Once we have followed this step, we must use every weapon that God has given us to walk in freedom.

For the weapons of our warfare are not carnal, but mighty through God to the pulling down of strongholds; Casting down imagination, and every high thing that exalteth itself against the knowledge of God, and bringing into

captivity every thought to the obedience of
Christ. (II Corinthians 10:4-5)

By using all that is available to us, including
the principles of God, we will have the strength to
overcome the world. In addition, we will have the
power to bring the flesh under control. And once
we have conquered the flesh, we can then move on
to the final battleground – the devil.

Section 3

▼

The Devil

Be self-controlled and alert. Your enemy, the devil, prowls around like a roaring lion looking for someone to devour. I Peter 5:8 NIV

The devil is real. His number one deception is to cause man not to believe in his existence. The Bible tells us otherwise. As believers, we must understand that we have an adversary. Because God is love, debates have been ongoing as to how He could create such an evil being who has wreaked havoc on the world. God created Lucifer in all righteousness, but he chose to become corrupt. If we are to overcome the enemy, we must know him.

Anyone in the military will tell you that the best weapon against an enemy is knowledge, not just force. By knowing their enemy, they can prepare themselves against their opponent's strength and exploit their weaknesses. Before examining ways to overcome the devil, we must understand who he is. We will look at his *creation, calamity,* and *conclusion.*

Creation

The devil's God-given name at his creation was Lucifer. Lucifer means "shining star or son of the morning." God created him as one of His archangels. The book of Ezekiel describes the beauty and honor bestowed upon Lucifer.

You were the model of perfection, full of wisdom and perfect in beauty. You were in Eden, the garden of God. Every precious stone adorned you: ruby, topaz and emerald, chrysolite, onyx and jasper, sapphire, turquoise and beryl. Your settings and mountings were made of gold; on the day you were created, they were prepared. You were anointed as a guardian cherub, for so I ordained you. You were on the holy mount of God and you walked among the fiery stones. You were blameless in your ways from the day you were created... (Ezekiel 28:12-15a NIV)

God made Lucifer perfect. He was anointed to stand by God and walk around the throne of God. He was a guardian cherub around the throne. He was full of wisdom and the perfection of beauty. He was one of God's chief angels and creation.

No other angels in the scripture are given such an awesome description, not even Michael or

Gabriel. God's anointing rested upon Lucifer and God had ordained it so. Lucifer was also present at creation for the text says he was in Eden, not as a serpent, but as the anointed cherub of God. When we look at all the things God had bestowed upon him, it is hard to believe that this is the one whom we now call our adversary.

What led to his fall? What caused the perfect, beautiful, and wise angel to fall into calamity (disaster or ruin)?

Calamity

Lucifer had it all. He was perfect in all of his ways, but he fell. Further reading of Ezekiel gives us insight into what caused his fall.

You were blameless in your ways, from the day you were created, till wickedness was found in you. Through your widespread trade, you were filled with violence, and you sinned. So, I drove you out in disgrace from the mount of God, and I expelled thee, O guardian cherub, from among the fiery stones. Your heart became proud on account of your beauty, and you corrupted your wisdom because of your splendor. (Ezekiel 28:15-17a)

Lucifer fell because of pride. He became puffed up because of his beauty. He became infatuated with himself and he "forgot" that he was only a creation. This is why Ezekiel said that his wisdom was corrupted.

Even though he understood he was only a creation of God, his splendor made him arrogant. The wisdom that God had given him was corrupted through pride. His thinking became warped and he began to worship his own beauty and splendor. He thought that he should be God. He even caused other angels to rebel against God and follow him.

How art thou fallen from heaven, O Lucifer, son of the morning! How art thou cut to the ground, which didst weak the nations! For thou hast said in thine heart, "I will ascend to heaven, I will exalt my throne above the stars of God, I will sit also upon the mount of the congregation in the sides of the north, I will ascend above the heights of the clouds, and I will be like the most High." (Isaiah 14:12-14 KJV)

Lucifer's plan was to take over. He had a list of things that he would do. He actually accomplished the first two. He already was present in heaven. Secondly, when he stated that he would exalt his throne above the stars of God, he meant he would exercise authority over the angels (stars) of God. He succeeded only in part because not all of the angels shared in his delusion. He allowed his beauty, perfection, and wisdom to cloud his judgment. He thought that he could overthrow God. This was his calamity or ruin. He deceived himself.

This should serve as a warning to us to be aware of pride. God has gifted many of us to be in His service. We must not allow the things that God has blessed us with to blind and corrupt us, or we will find ourselves walking in the way of Lucifer. Now that we have looked at his creation and calamity, let us now look at his conclusion or end.

Conclusion

The conclusion or end of Lucifer's story will not be fully achieved until the Day of Judgment. God has already exacted out his sentence in part. Michael, the archangel, cast

Lucifer and his followers out of heaven after their rebellion against God.

It is believed that the "third of the stars in heaven" that the tail of the red dragon cast down to the earth means that a third of the angels in heaven followed him (Revelation 12). After being cast out of heaven, his name was changed from Lucifer (shining star) to Satan, which means adversary or snake. He also is now known as the devil, meaning wicked one.

He had dominion in heaven as a guardian cherub. He had authority over some of the angels because he was the seal of perfection and beauty. Now, he is referred to as the prince of the power of the air (Ephesians 2:2). He went from representing the beauty and the presence of God to representing all that is evil. He now works to bring shame to God and His creation just as He worked to bring honor and glory to the Father in the beginning.

Though his destruction and end has not yet been realized, it will come. He will be thrown into the bottomless pit, first. He will be released and then cast into the lake of fire. He will be tormented for all eternity, not only because he caused man to sin, but also because he rebelled against God in the beginning. When this occurs, the conclusion to Lucifer's story will be complete.

Since we are made in God's likeness and image, he hates us just as much as he hates God. He has one mission in mind for mankind – seek and destroy. Our enemy is on his job daily. Because of this, the believer must pray continually and be watchful.

Jesus told the disciples to watch and pray. If they did not watch and pray, they would fall into temptation or into the hands of the evil one (Matthew 26:41). Satan and his fallen angels are at work continually to destroy and deceive men. In the book of Job, we discover what the enemy does daily. God asks the devil where he had been. His reply should cause us to be sober,

> *And the Lord said to Satan, "From where do you come?" Then Satan answered the Lord and said, "From roaming about on the earth and walking round on it. (Job 1:7)*

Our adversary and the fallen angles are constantly roaming the earth, searching for someone to devour. Why? They are in battle with God over the souls of men. The enemy will be judged in the last days; therefore, he wants to take as many of us as he can with him to the Judgment. Therefore, it behooves us to be on alert at all times. And at the same time, we must not be afraid.

God has given us power over the works of the enemy (Luke 10:19). The very reason Jesus came into the world was to destroy the works of the devil (I John 3:8). We find numerous examples in scripture confirming and reaffirming the believer's authority over Satan.

Through the Spirit of God, we will not be ignorant of Satan's tactics and schemes (II Corinthians 2:11). Though the Word is given to us a weapon against the enemy, many are still defeated by his tactics. We are defeated when we walk in ignorance. We must walk in wisdom.

Therefore, be careful how you walk, not as unwise men, but as wise, making the most of your time, because the days are evil. (Ephesians 5:15-16)

The reason we must walk in the wisdom and light of God because the days are evil. If we do not do this, we will be unwise in our decisions. We will become subject to the schemes of the enemy.

We must be aware of the tactics of the enemy. However, we cannot combat his tactics if we do not know what they are.

The enemy uses three main schemes against believers. If we were to examine our walks with God, we would find that the enemy has fought us often and we did not realize it. They are as follows: 1) distraction, 2) deception, and 3) desire.

Distraction

One commonly used expression is, "You can't see the forest because of the trees." This expression says that a person does not recognize the vastness of the forest because he is preoccupied with each individual tree. How does this relate to us?

The enemy pulls us away from God, one tree at a time. While we are focused on one area (tree) in our life, another problem area springs up because we are not being watchful. One of the enemy's main tactics is to cause distraction.

While we are distracted, he begins to work on other areas in our lives unhindered. In I Samuel chapters 27 through 30, we are given an account of David fleeing from King Saul out of Israel. He then forms an allegiance with the Philistines.

With him, he brings 2 wives, 600 men, and their households. It is important to note that the Philistines were considered an enemy of Israel and God. Once David arrives, one of the lords of the Philistines, named Achish, finds favor in him. He even gives David the city, Ziklag.

David fights battles alongside the Philistines. His goal was to use the Philistines to help him kill off some other enemies of Israel. As the story continues, we are told that just before they go into battle against Israel, some of the princes of the Philistines distrust David. Achish sends David back to Ziklag because of this. Upon his return, however, he and his men discover that their city has been invaded and their belongings taken, including wives and children.

In this story, David thought himself smart. He would join with the Philistines and wipe out some of his enemies. His plan seemed to work at first, and then it fails. He was so busy fighting alongside the Philistines that he did not know there were plans against him. He paid no attention to his enemies because he focused on the Philistines only. He suffered loss, but God was gracious to let him and his men recover all.

As believers, we must not fall into this trap. We cannot become focused on one thing and lose control over other things. We cannot allow our families and friends to distract us from God. We cannot even allow church work or service to be our focus.

Even things we do for Christ cannot become more important than our relationship with Him. If this happens, we will fall into the hands of the enemy. We read in the gospels of how Martha worked in the kitchen when Jesus came and how Mary sat at his feet,

> *Now as they were traveling along, he entered into a certain village; and a woman name Martha welcomed Him into her home. And she had a sister called Mary, who moreover was listening to the Lord's word, seated at His feet. But Martha was distracted with all of her preparations; and she came up to Him and said, "Lord, do you not care that my sister has left me to do all the serving alone? Then tell her to help me?" But the Lord answered her and said*

*to her, "Martha, Martha, you are worried
and bothered about so many things; but
only a few things are necessary, really only
one, for Mary has chosen the good part,
which shall not be taken away from her."
(Luke 10:38-42 Emphasis mine)*

Martha thought she was doing the right
thing, but Jesus corrected her. She was so
distracted trying to serve the Lord, that she was
neglecting fellowship with Him. We must learn
from Jesus' words. We, oftentimes, become
distracted with many of life's concerns and
problems. We also become overly concerned with
trying to serve the Lord that we miss out on the
blessings of fellowship with Him. In this state, we
will be vulnerable to an attack of the enemy.

Distractions will cause us to be frustrated
like Martha. She could not appreciate and enjoy
the presence of Jesus in her home because of it. As

believers, we sometimes do not enjoy our salvation because we are too busy with concerns.

Martha responded in the wrong spirit due to her frustration. If we are not careful, our distractions will cause irritation and frustration. Moreover, frustration will cause us to respond negatively to life and to Christ. Martha rebuked Christ and complained about her sister not helping her. We, too, will develop the same attitude and think that God is to blame for our frustration. In this state, we are crippled and cannot move forward in God. The enemy's plan would have worked. Therefore, we must not allow distraction, in any form, to put us in bondage. It is only a tool of the enemy. We must submit all of our cares unto Christ, as instructed in the scriptures. Jesus said,

Come unto me, all who are weary and heavy-laden, and I will give you rest. Take my yoke upon you, and learn from me, for

I am gentle and humble in heart; and you shall find rest for your souls. For my yoke is easy and my load is light. (Matthew 11:28-30)

It is also written,

Cast all your anxiety on him because he cares for you. (I Peter 5:7 NIV)

And again,

Thou wilt keep him in perfect peace, who mind is stayed on thee: because he trusteth in thee. (Isaiah 26:3 KJV)

If we allow the Word of God to govern our lives and the peace of God to guard our hearts, the enemy will not be able to use distractions to keep us from walking in victory. Let us keep our thoughts and minds focused on the Lord.

Deception

One of the most powerful tools of the enemy is deception. Throughout the scriptures, we find examples of men and women falling into this trap. Eve was deceived in the Garden. She ate of the forbidden fruit and gave some to her husband. The Israelites were deceived. They thought that God would not judge them for their sins. They continued in sin until they felt the wrath of God.

Even in Jesus' day, the Pharisees were deceived. They thought that true righteousness could only come through the law and its rituals. Therefore, when Jesus came, they could not receive Him because they were blinded. Their deception led to the crucifixion of the Lord Jesus.

If we are not alert, deception will also lead to the death of Christ in us. Our relationship with God will be hindered and at best, stagnant. In numerous scriptures, Jesus warned His disciples against being deceived. He warned them of false prophets and teachers that would emerge.

Paul warned believers not to be carried away with fables and warped teachings. There are too many warning given in scripture for us to not be on guard. As we proceed, we will look at the cause of deception and how to avoid this tool of the enemy.

As soon as we hear the word "deception," the only things we think of are cults, erroneous teachings, and false prophets. Therefore, Christians will believe that they are exempt. They do not understand that deception can occur in subtle ways. For instance, when we do not believe that God will heal us, we are deceived. The scriptures tell us that God will heal His people.

By not knowing the scriptures, believers will settle for all that the enemy will bring into their lives. Along with knowing the scriptures, a knowledge and belief in the power of God is necessary. Oftentimes, we believe the scriptures, but do not believe that God will perform miracles and blessings for us, as He did then. This also is another form of deception.

We believe that God can deliver others; yet, when it comes to the power of God being activated in our individual lives, there is a struggle. We must not only hold to the truth of the scripture, but also believe that the God of the scripture is willing to manifest His power in our lives. We must know the scripture and believe in the power of God. If not, the enemy will keep us in bondage. Our walk with God will seem futile and lifeless.

The Sadducees presented a question to Jesus. They wanted to test Him. Through their story, they wanted to prove that there was no resurrection of the dead. We must first understand that the Sadducees were Jews. They were instructed as the Pharisees were, yet, they were deceived. The Pharisees, though bound by tradition, maintained belief in the supernatural and the resurrection of the dead. These things were proven valid under the law. The Sadducees, however, had been deceived into thinking that none of those things were valid. After their inquiry, Jesus responds,

Jesus replied, "Are you not in error because you do not know the scriptures or the power of God?" (Mark 12:24)

He told them that they were in error (deception). The question they posed was a product of their deception. From His response to them, we find an answer to how a believer may fall into deception. Jesus gave two reasons as to why they were deceived. These two reasons apply to us today.

The first was that they did not know the scriptures, and the second was that they did not know the power of God. When the believer does not know the scriptures or the power of God, the enemy will bring him into deception.

We stated earlier that the devil is now referred to as the "prince of the power of the air." This tells us that his tactics resemble the air. We know that air cannot be seen, but its influence can be seen all around. Looking at objects and how they move help us to determine wind (air) direction.

Sometimes air can be hot or cold and it can be thick or thin. We must understand that even though we cannot see the "prince," he is at work for we need only to look at his effects. His influence is seen in television, heard on the radio, and even felt and seen in the Church. We are warned to be alert. He has released a host of spirits to deceive us.

But the Spirit explicitly says that in the later times some will fall away from the faith, paying attention to deceitful spirits and doctrines of demons. (I Timothy 4:1)

It is in these times that believers have to be careful not to fall away from the Church and the faith. Deceitful spirits have been sent to take us away from the faith. Paul states that believers will pay attention to the doctrines of demons. We know that a doctrine is a teaching.

Demons have been taught of the devil and will try to put their teachings into the hearts of man. We must be careful not to be carried away with demonic doctrine and those who teach them. Jesus stated,

For false Christ's and false prophets will arise and will show you great wonders, to mislead, if possible, even the elect. (Matthew 24:24)

Men and women will not only teach demonic doctrine, but will have signs following. All of this is done in order to lead the elect or chosen one into apostasy. It will be possible for us to be deceived if we make it possible. We must ask God for eyes to see and ears to hear.

The Word brings stability, while the power of God brings life. Without both of these, the enemy will keep us blinded. We will become subject to false teachings. We will not be able to live in faith. Our relationship with God will become stagnant and lifeless. In this state, we will believe every lie that the enemy will bring to mind, about God and ourselves. In order to overcome deception, we must draw to God through the Word and trust that His power will operate in our lives.

Desire

Above distraction and deception, there is only one tool that the enemy uses most frequently. He uses the desires present in our flesh to overcome us. He uses our lusts and weaknesses against us. We stated earlier that the enemy does not make us sin, but he will exploit our inward compulsions.

During His earthly ministry, Jesus used parables to teach the disciples. He used everyday examples to explain the principles of the Kingdom of God. One of the most celebrated parables is that of the farmer that went out to sow seed (Matthew 13:1-9, 18-23).

Within this parable, we can see how the enemy exploits our desires and weaknesses, using them to attack us. The parable details for us where a seed may land when thrown by a farmer: *by the wayside, upon stony places, among thorns,* and *upon good ground.* Jesus stated that all of these places represented those who heard the Word. Of these four mentioned, the first three areas might also indicate specific areas in a believer's life that the enemy will exploit in order to dominate him.

Some Seeds Fell By The Wayside...

The first illustration Jesus used to describe where some seeds fell was by the wayside.

And when he sowed, some seeds fell by the wayside, and the fowls of the air came and devoured them up. (Matthew 13:4 KJV)

The consequence of falling by the wayside was that the birds of the air came down and devoured them. Jesus said this referred to those who received the Word, but at some point, the enemy came and snatched it away from them (Matthew 13:18). Let us consider how this illustrates an attack of the enemy.

The wayside can also represent an unguarded area in our lives for which we have not built up a defense. This, in turn, leaves an opening for an attack of the enemy. In the parable, the only reason the birds could get to the seeds is that they were out in the open without protection.

We find many believers have certain desires that constantly entrap them. In addition, they have weaknesses for which they have no power to resist. They live in defeat, dominated by desire. Many are in despair of ever gaining the victory. Even though they pray and hear sermons, they do not find deliverance. For when they hear the sermons, the enemy comes immediately and snatches the Word that they heard.

How does the enemy snatch the Word from the believer? He accomplishes it through fear, doubt, and unbelief. With these tools, the enemy paralyzes the believer. He, inevitably, gives in to his desire and does not resist. This leads to the enemy stealing the Word.

Fear

The first tactic used by the devil is fear. The enemy uses fear to deceive the believer into thinking that he will never be delivered. Fear is what kept all of the disciple, except Peter, from walking on water (Matthew 14:29). When a believer walks in fear, he will not walk in faith and in power. Peter knew that water was unstable, yet, he trusted Jesus enough to overcome that knowledge. Though we may have weaknesses, if we walk in faith, we can walk over them, even as Peter walked on the water. When fear of failure is in a believer, he will doubt that he can be delivered. He will feel that it is impossible. Every time an impure thought arises in a person bound by fear, he will run in fear.

In one passage of scripture, the devil is compared to a roaring lion (I Peter 5:8). A lion roars in order to strike fear in its prey. Amos the prophet asked a question, "A lion has roared! Who will not fear (Amos 3:8)?" How does the devil roar? He brings thoughts and desires to the mind. When this occurs, the believer must not become afraid or discouraged. If he does, the enemy causes him to think that because the thought or desire surfaced, he is not delivered.

He is deceived in his thinking. Consequently, he will fulfill the desire, feeling that he is bound and has no other option. He believes the lie, "I thought it, and that is just as bad as doing it." Do not be fooled. It is easier to get over an impure thought than an impure action. Thoughts can be forgotten, but the flesh has to be brought under control. You must remember that you have the power to resist temptation.

Every believer should follow the popular slogan used in the world when faced with temptation, "Just Say No!" We must not be bound by fear, but remember what Paul told Timothy,

> *For God did not give us the spirit of timidity – of cowardice, of crave and cringing and fawning fear – but [He has given us a spirit] of power and of love and of a calm and well-balanced mind and discipline and self-control. (II Timothy 1:7 Amplified)*

Doubt

The second tactic the enemy uses to steal the Word from the believer is doubt. The enemy uses doubt to dominate the believer by making him unsure of his deliverance. When confidence in deliverance is present, the enemy comes to bring doubt. Doubt causes you to be unstable in your mind. It causes you to be double-minded. In this state, you cannot receive deliverance. Moreover, if you try to lay hold of deliverance, it will be in vain.

But when he asks, he must believe and not doubt, because he who doubts is like a wave of the sea, blown and tossed by the wind. That man should not think he would receive anything from the Lord; he is a double-minded man, unstable in all his ways. (James 1:6-8 NIV)

When we pray for deliverance, we must first believe that we can be delivered. If we begin to doubt, our path to deliverance will be hindered. Peter did not last very long on top of the water. He began to doubt because of the waves. As long as the devil keeps us in doubt of our ability to walk in deliverance, we will be defeated.

The believer must realize that doubt and double-mindedness is not just a train of thought, but a condition of the heart. True faith and belief come from the heart (Romans 10:10). Doubt is a sin and should be treated as such.

> *Draw near to God and he will draw near to you. Cleanse your hands, you sinners; and purify your hearts, you double-minded. (James 4:8)*

The believer must ask for forgiveness for having doubt in his heart, and move towards faith. Once faith is exercised, it will bring deliverance.

> *And Jesus answered and said to them, "Truly I say unto you, if you have faith,*

and do not doubt, you shall not only do what was done to the fig tree, but even if you say to this mountain, 'Be taken up and cast into the sea,' it shall happen." *(Matthew 21:21)*

Jesus told His disciples and us that if we would believe and not doubt, anything is possible (Mark 9:23). Walking in deliverance is possible through faith. Even in areas where we may have had struggles for years, we will have the victory if we exercise faith.

Unbelief

The third tactic used by the enemy to steal the Word from our hearts is unbelief. Unbelief is one of the most powerful weapons used by the devil. Unbelief closes every door to the possibility of deliverance. Even if a believer operates in fear and doubt, they know that deliverance is possible though they may not feel they can obtain it.

Unbelief, however, means there is no hope. Thomas, one of the twelve, received the title "Doubting Thomas" because he did not believe that Jesus was resurrected. His title should have been "Unbelieving Thomas." He did not just doubt that Jesus was alive; he did not believe it at all. It was only through the love and mercy of God that Christ revealed Himself unto him.

> *But Thomas, one of the twelve, called Didymus, was not with them when Jesus came. The other disciples therefore were saying to him, "We have seen the Lord!" But he said to them, "Unless I shall see in his hands the imprint of the nails, and put my hands into his side, I Will Not Believe." (John 20:24-25 Emphasis Mine)*

Thomas walked with Jesus and saw the miracles.

Jesus told him and the others that He would rise again, but he did not believe. Those found in unbelief will always look for something to make them believe. Even though they may have seen or heard, they want something that they can put their hands on.

Unbelief blocks the believer from receiving help. He will say there is no hope. The only hope for someone bound by unbelief is the mercy of God. To be delivered from this deception, God must reveal Himself, even as Christ did to Thomas (John 20:26). Until the believer learns to combat fear, doubt, and unbelief, the enemy will always come and snatch the Word of deliverance from him.

Some Fell Upon Rocky Places…

The second illustration Jesus used was that some seeds fell upon stony places, without much soil.

And others fell upon the rocky places,
where they did not have much soil; and
immediately they sprang up, because they
had no depth of soil. But when the sun had
risen, they were scorched; and because
they had no root, they withered away.
(Matthew 13:5-6)

The seeds that fell on rocks sprouted quickly
because they had no root. Therefore, when the sun
came up, they were burned and were dried up.
Jesus said that this referred to those who received
the Word with joy, but had no foundation.
Subsequently, when persecution and tribulation
arose, they became overwhelmed and gave up
(Matthew 13:31).

A closer examination of these verses shows
us that these "rocky places" could also represent

those areas in the believer's life where there is a constant battle, making them targets for the enemy. Since there is a struggle, the believer is always looking for help and an answer.

Therefore, when they hear the Word preached, they quickly say that they are delivered or set free. They deceive themselves because they do not take the time to apply the Word to their weak areas. They do not allow the Word to take root in their hearts. Therefore, when the desire or temptation returns, they cannot handle it and give up. The Word they heard did not have much soil to grow in.

When we claim deliverance prematurely, we set ourselves up for defeat. We will become utterly discouraged and disappointed because we thought we were free when we were not. The enemy will use this to keep us in bondage and to cause us to lose hope of being delivered. We must not be like those in the parable. We must allow the Word to settle in us and grow before we claim complete deliverance.

And Some Fell Among Thorns...

The third illustration that Jesus used was that some seeds fell among the thorns.

And others fell among the thorns, and the thorns came up and choked them out. (Matthew 13:7)

The consequence of these landing among thorns was that the thorns choked them. Jesus said that this referred to those who received the Word, but the cares of the world consume him, making him unfruitful (Matthew 31:22).

Let us consider the above in this manner: the thorns may represent known areas of sin and compromise in the believer's life. We understand that the seeds and thorns were in the same ground. They each need soil to grow. Nevertheless, in Jesus' parable, the thorns prevailed. This is indicative of the believer who hears the Word consistently, but chooses not to apply the Word to his life. The enemy deceives him into thinking that it is O.K. and God understands.

This believer fought for deliverance and victory in the beginning. However, when he saw that God did not judge him harshly and was patient with him, he decided not to try anymore.

These types of believers feel that since God still blesses them and is with them, then their sin cannot be all that bad. They manipulate the concept that God loves us just as we are. They do not understand that God will love us the way that we are until we become who we are supposed to be in Him. Thus, they attend Church and fellowship with believers. They will even grow in the knowledge of God, but their areas of sin will also grow and eventually dominate them.

Ultimately, their desires and the cares of this life control them, making them unfruitful in the kingdom of God. These are believers who hear the Word, but will not change. In this case, there is no conflict with the enemy because they are his to manipulate.

We have seen that the enemy only has three main tactics: distraction, deception, and desire. His most successful tactic is man's sinful desires. It is what he uses most to keep us from living a victorious Christian life. The enemy keeps the believer in bondage by exploiting his desires and weaknesses.

If he keeps us wrestling with our flesh, we will never overcome. However, once the tools of the enemy are discovered, we need to know what to do. If someone asked you right now about the areas where you are having trouble, you could give them an answer immediately. However, knowing the problem without a solution is useless and frustrating. We will now look at ways to overcome the enemy and his tactics. Only then can we live in victory.

In the introduction, we looked at the process Jesus went through to overcome the world, the flesh, and the devil. Had Jesus failed, he would have compromised his position given to Him by God. His victory was important to us all. Though tempted by the devil, he was able to resist. By fasting, He gained control over His flesh and went on to defeat the tactics of the enemy.

Jesus defeated the enemy using the Word of God and prayer. Along with these two weapons, we must add praise. If we follow Jesus' example and give praise unto God, we will overcome the enemy and walk in victory.

The Word of God

When Jesus was tested by the devil, He used the Word to combat him. We must also use the Word. We must not only quote the scriptures, but also believe in them. We must believe the scriptures and be dedicated to the study and application of the Word to everyday life. If we will not do this, we will be defeated. We must have the Word and the entire armor that God has given us.

Therefore, take up the full armor of God, that you may be able to resist in the evil day, and have done all, stand firm therefore, having girded your loins with truth, and having put on the breastplate of righteousness, and having shod your feet with the preparation of the gospel of peace.

In addition to all, take up the shield of faith with which you will be able to extinguish all the flaming missiles of the evil one. And take the helmet of salvation, and the sword of the Spirit, which is the word of God. (Ephesians 6:11-17)

We need every part of the armor if we are going to stand against the enemy. The girdle or belt of truth is needed. It helps to hold everything that He has given us together. Because God is truth, we can trust in everything that He has said or promised. In addition, we need to be people of truth.

The breastplate of righteousness is most crucial. It helps us to identify with the righteousness of Christ. Though we are sinners and He was righteous, He became as a sinner and we took on His righteousness. The breastplate protects our hearts and keeps us from being defiled by sin and the flesh.

Our feet must be sandaled with the preparation of the gospel of peace. This means we ought to stand in readiness to take the gospel with us everywhere, and be led by peace.

The shield of faith is needed for your protection. Without faith, the rest of the armor will not hold up long. Our faith in God is what keeps us fighting through tests, trials, and other attacks of the enemy.

The helmet of salvation is needed so that the believer will be certain of his salvation. The helmet is used as a shield against the lies and tactics that the enemy brings to mind. Finally, we need the sword or the Word. It is used when we want to take the offensive against the enemy.

All of the pieces of armor listed, except the "sword of the Spirit," are forms of defense. Although they can protect, they do not make effective weapons. Moreover, the only offensive weapon given to us is the sword, or the Word of God. Many believe that faith is the most powerful weapon against the enemy. How untrue! Faith cannot even be gained except through the Word.

So, faith comes by hearing, and hearing by the Word of God. (Romans 10:17)

Faith is most important in our walk with God, but the Word is crucial in fighting. It alone is the ultimate weapon against the enemy. When Jesus was confronted by the devil, He did not say, "I have faith," but he declared, "It is written!" Through the Word, we know what power and authority we have, and how to exercise it. If we know, understand, and apply the Word, we will defeat the enemy.

Alongside the Word, prayer is essential. We discussed earlier of how prayer combined with fasting brought control over the flesh. The same is true concerning prayer and use of the Word. Prayer increases the power of the Word in our lives. Jesus prayed and fasted for forty days and nights and then He rose up and used the Word to defeat the enemy.

Along with possessing the armor, Paul exhorts the Ephesians to pray and intercede. Paul understood that prayer is what gives the armor its effectiveness and strength. Without prayer, the armor is less effective.

And pray in the Spirit on all occasions with all kinds of prayers and requests. With this in mind, be alert and always keep on praying for all the saints. (Ephesians 6:18)

Paul states that we must not only pray, but also pray in the Spirit. Only then will our warfare against the enemy be most effective. Primary is the

Word of God, and second is prayer. Both are effective offenses against the devil. Prayer alongside the Word forms a weapon more powerful than any two-edged sword in the hands of the believer.

For the word of God is living and active and sharper than any two-edged sword, and piercing as far as the division of soul and spirit, of both joints and marrow, and able to judge the thoughts and intentions of the heart. And there is no creature hidden from His sight, but all things are open and lay bare to the eyes of Him with whom we have to do. (Hebrews 4:12-13)

The Word in action penetrates through all of the devices of the enemy. In order for the Word to perform its function, the believer must understand how to apply it. This is accomplished through the study of the Word.

Study and be eager and do your utmost to present yourself to God approved (tested by trial), a workman who has no cause to be ashamed, correctly analyzing and accurately dividing – rightly handling and skillfully teaching the word of truth. But avoid all empty (vain, useless, and idle) talk, for it will lead people into more and more ungodliness. (II Timothy 2:15-16 Amplified)

Paul told Timothy to study that he would know how to apply the Word. This is so he would be able to avoid empty talk. Why? Foolish talk leads to more ungodliness; meaning, it will cause you to operate in the flesh. And if you operate in the flesh, the enemy is sure to keep you in bondage. The Word teaches us how to keep the flesh under control while serving as our primary weapon against the enemy. Thus, to ensure victory, the Word of God must be active in our lives.

Praise

We have another weapon that can be used at any time. You need neither a complete understanding of the Bible, nor knowledge of how to say lofty prayers. It is the weapon of praise. Both Old and New Testaments attest to the fact that God seeks our praise. In addition, we learn that it is our responsibility to give Him praise. Why?

God does not need our praise for He has angels in heaven that fly before the throne continually giving Him honor and glory. When we praise God, it is a sign of our appreciation for all that He has done. In addition, praise can be an awesome force against the enemy.

Jehoshaphat and Jerusalem

King Jehoshaphat had a problem. Three

nations gathered to fight against Judah. II Chronicles 20 gives us an account of how the Moabites and Ammonites (both long standing enemies of Israel) and the inhabitants of mount Seir joined forces to overthrow Judah. Jehoshaphat was afraid and sought the Lord. The Holy Spirit came upon Jahaziel, the son of Zechariah and he prophesied saying,

Hearken ye, all Judah, and ye inhabitants of Jerusalem, and thou king Jehoshaphat, Thus saith the Lord unto you, Be not afraid nor dismayed by reason of this great multitude; for the battle is not yours, but God's. To morrow go ye down against them: behold, they come up by the cliff of Ziz; and ye shall find them at the end of the brook, before the wilderness of Jeruel. Ye shall not need to fight in this battle: set yourselves, stand ye still, and see the salvation of the Lord with you, O Judah

and Jerusalem: fear not, nor be dismayed;
to morrow go out against them: for the
Lord will be with you. (II Chronicles
20:15-17)

They were told not to fight, but still go out against their enemies. Oftentimes, when we are faced with opposition from all sides, it seems like there is no response from God. In spite of these things, we know we have to face the situation.

When Jehoshaphat heard the prophetic word, he knew what to do on the next day. He understood that if they could not fight and win, they could praise and watch God be God. When they arose the next day, he set the singers in front to praise God. Look at what happens as they began to praise,

And when they began to sing and to praise,
the Lord set ambushments against the

children of Ammon, Moab, and mount Seir, which were come against Judah; and they were smitten. For the children of Ammon and Moab stood up against the inhabitants of mount Seir, utterly to slay and destroy them: and when they had made an end of the inhabitants of Seir, every one helped to destroy another. (II Chronicles 20:22-23 KJV)

We find here that when they began to praise, God heard from heaven and fought for them. When facing overwhelming situations, we must remember that praise touches the heart of God. It is a sweet-smelling odor in His nostrils. The scriptures say that God inhabits the praise of His people Israel, and we now are His chosen people. As we praise, God's presence and power manifests. When this occurs, the forces of darkness must flee. If we learn to praise, we will allow God to fight for us.

Joshua and Jericho

Another well-known account of how praise to God brought deliverance over an enemy is the story of Jericho. After crossing over into Canaan, Israel had come to Jericho, which was surrounded by a wall. The Lord gave instructions. They did not have to break down the wall. The only thing they had to do was march around the wall, play instruments, and shout unto God. When they gave the final shout of praise and victory, it produced results.

So the people shouted when the priests blew with the trumpets: and it came to pass, when the people heard the sound of the trumpet, and the people shouted with a great shout, that the wall fell down flat, so that the people went up into the city, every man straight before him, and they took the city. (Joshua 6:20 KJV)

We should follow their example. When we come to our own personal Jericho walls, we must shout unto God in praise and watch as our walls fall down and we conquer every obstacle that is set against us.

Paul, Silas, and the Philippi Jail

Finally, we will look at another familiar account of how praise brought deliverance. In the book of Acts chapter 16, we read of how Paul and Silas preached the gospel at Philippi with results.

And on the Sabbath we went out of the city by a river side, where prayer was wont to be made; and we sat down, and spake unto the women which resorted thither. And a certain woman named Lydia, a seller of purple, of the city of Thyatira, which worshipped God, heard us: whose heart the

Lord opened, that she attended unto the things which were spoken of Paul. And when she was baptized, and her household, she besought us, saying, If ye have judged me to be faithful to the Lord, come into my house, and abide there. And she constrained us. (Acts 16:13-15 KJV)

Next, we find that a woman with a spirit of divination followed the apostles around as they preach. It is interesting to note here that it seems as if every time there is a success in God, the enemy comes to withstand it.

And it came to pass, as we went to prayer, a certain damsel possessed with a spirit of divination met us, which brought her masters much gain by soothsaying: The same followed Paul and us, and cried, saying, These men are the servants of the most high God, which shew unto us the way of salvation. (Acts 16:16-17 KJV)

The enemy tried to ally himself with the men of God in order to bring a reproach to the name of God. But Paul, being sensitive to the Spirit of God, confronts that spirit and ends up in jail along with Silas.

> *And this did she many days. But Paul, being grieved, turned and said to the spirit, I command thee in the name of Jesus Christ to come out of her. And he came out the same hour. And when her masters saw that the hope of their gains was gone, they caught Paul and Silas, and drew them into the marketplace unto the rulers, And brought them to the magistrates, saying, These men, being Jews, do exceedingly trouble our city, And teach customs, which are not lawful for us to receive, neither to observe, being Romans.*

And the multitude rose up together against them: and the magistrates rent off their clothes, and commanded to beat them. And when they had laid many stripes upon them, they cast them into prison, charging the jailor to keep them safely. (Acts 16:18-23 KJV)

Paul and Silas were in jail, bound both hand and foot along with other prisoners. Now, let us look at how praise brought forth deliverance from their captors.

And at midnight Paul and Silas prayed, and sang praises unto God: and the prisoners heard them. And suddenly there was a great earthquake, so that the foundations of the prison were shaken: and immediately all the doors were opened, and every one's bands were loosed. (Acts 16:25-26 KJV)

When Paul and Silas prayed and sang praise unto God, what was the result? The result was freedom from their enemy. If we would learn to praise God in our "midnights," we leave ourselves open for God to shake the very foundation of the adversary in our circumstances.

Interestingly enough, their praise also brought deliverance to the others in the prison. Our praise will do the same, if we would learn to give thanks in all things. We must remember that our praise can be an instrument of destruction against all the works and tactics of the enemy.

Though God has given us the Word of God, prayer, and praise as weapons against the enemy, we must not give up before victory is achieved. Believers will fight and stand against the enemy; but when some do not see the results of their warfare, they stop fighting. We must remember to persevere until the end. Paul stated that he had to press toward the mark.

Brethren, I count not myself to have apprehended: but this one thing I do, forgetting those things which are behind, and reaching forth unto those things which are before, I press toward the mark for the prize of the high calling of God in Christ Jesus. (Philippians 3:13-14)

We, too, must press and endure until the end. Do not give up if no results are seen immediately. When Israel crossed over into Canaan, they did not possess the land all at once. They fought daily. As they fought each individual battle and won, they gained control over more of the land.

Do not try to be perfect in one day, but each day win a victory. With each victory, you will gain more ground in your walk with God and go to living victoriously. Not only do we have to press, but also endure all that will come up against us while we are striving to walk in victory. Paul instructed Timothy to endure hardness as a good soldier.

Endure hardness, as a good soldier of Jesus Christ, along with me. No man that is in a war entangles himself with the affairs of this life, that he may please him who has chosen him to be a soldier. (II Timothy 2:3-4)

Our battle against the devil is real and sometimes it will get hard. Nevertheless, if we endure the hard times, we will come out victorious. We must not faint, for at an appointed time, we will reap the benefits of our labor in Christ.

And let us not lose heart in doing good, for in due time we shall reap, if we do not grow weary. (Galatians 6:9)

In order for us to defeat the enemy, we must use the resources God has given us. If we would only give ourselves over to the study and application of the Word and become consistent in prayer, we will overcome the evil one. We must again remember that our praises carry the presence of God and are effective in warfare. We do not need formulas, just action.

An expression in the world says, "An ounce of prevention is worth a pound of cure." If we would be consistent in the Word and prayer in the beginning, the enemy's attack would not be so hard to resist or overcome. However, if we remember the Word, Prayer, and Praise, the plan of the enemy will be cancelled in our lives. And once his plans are defeated, he (the devil) is defeated. When we have conquered him, we can then live victoriously in Christ.

▼

Living Victoriously in Christ

And this is the victory that has overcome the world – our faith. (I John 5:4b)

The Way of Faith

The Word tells us that whatever and whosoever is born of God overcomes. As believers, we are predestined to overcome. No matter what obstacles stand in our way because of the world, the flesh, and the devil, we will have the victory. Though we are destined to overcome, our faith secures this victory.

If we try to face the world, the flesh, and the devil without faith, our efforts will be useless. We will not have the confidence to press on when there are failures and setbacks. As long as we maintain faith in God, we will overcome. Therefore, our faith must be developed and exercised along with our efforts to overcome. One thing we have to keep in mind is that faith does not begin with us; it begins with God.

For I say, through the grace given unto me, to every man that is among you, not to think of himself more highly than he ought to think; but to think soberly, according as God hath dealt to every man the measure of faith. (Romans 12:3 KJV)

God gives to every man a measure of faith. It is then up to us to develop that faith. We shall ask now, "What is faith?" The world defines faith as belief or trust without asking for proof. The Word describes faith on this wise,

Now faith is the assurance (the confirmation, the title deed) of things [we] hope for, being the proof of things [we] do not see and the conviction of their reality – faith perceiving as real fact what is not revealed to the senses. (Hebrews 11:1 Amplified)

Our faith in God guarantees that we will have whatever it is we are hoping for. In relation to living in victory, our faith tells us that we already have it. Even if we are experiencing defeat and failures while trying to overcome, faith dictates that we will win.

We must remember that overcoming is not just a one-time experience. It is something to be achieved on a daily basis. Even when we do not feel victorious, we must believe that we are. Our faith in God is what holds everything together. The scriptures tell us that we must live by faith. Once we have fought to gain ground in our walks with God, we cannot draw back.

But my righteous one shall live by faith; and if he shrinks back, my soul has no pleasure in him. (Hebrews 10:38)

We cannot afford to slow down in our pursuit of God and His holiness. If we do, our flesh will rule our lives and we will fall prey to the schemes of the enemy. It may seem that it is too hard or stressful to maintain success. Nevertheless, if our faith remains in tact, we will always come out on top. The secret to victorious living is maintaining your faith in God. After you have done all you can, stand in faith.

You must believe that you can overcome. Though we hear it in sermons and songs, we still think that we can only overcome once we die. While we are on this earth and in these mortal bodies, we can live in victory. Jesus said that all things are possible to them that believe. When you walk in faith, it does not matter how many times you have tried and failed.

Faith causes you to overcome every setback and disappointment. This will enable you to endure until victory is achieved. And, the God of your faith will strengthen, establish, and settle you. He will make you perfect in Him. Let us never give up in our quest to be conquerors in this life. Let us hold fast to the Word and the God of the Word. We will live victoriously in Christ.

As we strive to live a life of victory, let us remember the prayers that Paul made for the saints and ask that God will do the same for us:

I pray that the God of our Lord Jesus Christ, the Father of glory, may give to you a spirit of wisdom and of revelation in the knowledge of him. I pray that the eyes of your heart may be enlightened, so that you may know what is the hope of his calling, what are the riches of the glory of His inheritance in the saints. I pray that you would be strengthened with power through his Spirit in the inner man, so that Christ may dwell in your hearts through faith. I also pray that you may walk in a manner worthy of the Lord, to please him in all respects, bearing fruit in every good work and increasing in the knowledge of God. I pray that you would be strengthened with all power, according to his glorious might, for the attaining of steadfastness, and patience; joyously giving thanks to the Father, who has qualified us to share in the inheritance of the saints in light. (Ephesians 1:17-18; Ephesians 3:16-17; Colossians 1:10-12)

We will overcome if we walk in faith, apply the Word, and deny ourselves. Jesus overcame the world and so can we. The enemy has deceived us long enough. If the same Spirit that was in Christ is in us, we can overcome as He did. In our pursuit of God, let us persevere with patience. Remember, you *can* and *will* overcome the world, the flesh, and the devil, and live victoriously in Christ.

Appendix

In each section of the book, references were made to numerous scriptural accounts. Included here is the section where the references were made, the full account, and where it can be found in scripture.

INTRODUCTION

Temptation of Jesus – Matthew 4:1-11

1. Then was Jesus led up of the Spirit into the wilderness to be tempted of the devil.

2. And when he had fasted forty days and forty nights, he was afterward an hungered.

3. And when the tempter came to him, he said, If thou be the Son of God, command that these stones be made bread.

4. But he answered and said, It is written, Man shall not live by bread alone, but by every word that proceedeth out of the mouth of God.

5. Then the devil taketh him up into the holy city, and setteth him on a pinnacle of the temple,

6. And saith unto him, If thou be the Son of God, cast thyself down: for it is written, He shall give his angels charge concerning thee: and in their hands they shall bear thee up, lest at any time thou dash thy foot against a stone.

7. Jesus said unto him, It is written again, Thou shalt not tempt the Lord thy God.

8. Again, the devil taketh him up into an exceeding high mountain, and sheweth him all the kingdoms of the world, and the glory of them;

9. And saith unto him, All these things will I give thee, if thou wilt fall down and worship me.

10. Then saith Jesus unto him, Get thee hence, Satan: for it is written, Thou shalt worship the Lord thy God, and him only shalt thou serve.

11. Then the devil leaveth him, and, behold, angels came and ministered unto him.

SECTION 1 –THE WORLD

David & Bathsheba – II Samuel 11:1-27

1. And it came to pass, after the year was expired, at the time when kings go forth to battle, that David sent Joab, and his servants with him, and all Israel; and they destroyed the children of Ammon, and besieged Rabbah. But David tarried still at Jerusalem.

2. And it came to pass in an eveningtide, that David arose from off his bed, and walked upon the roof of the king's house: and from the roof he saw a woman washing herself; and the woman was very beautiful to look upon.

3. And David sent and inquired after the woman. And one said, Is not this Bathsheba, the daughter of Eliam, the wife of Uriah the Hittite?

4. And David sent messengers, and took her; and she came in unto him, and he lay with her; for she was purified from her uncleanness: and she returned unto her house.

5. And the woman conceived, and sent and told David, and said, I am with child.

6. And David sent to Joab, saying, Send me Uriah the Hittite. And Joab sent Uriah to David.

7. And when Uriah was come unto him, David demanded of him how Joab did, and how the people did, and how the war prospered.

8. And David said to Uriah, Go down to thy house, and wash thy feet. And Uriah departed out of the king's house, and there followed him a mess of meat from the king.

9. But Uriah slept at the door of the king's house with all the servants of his lord, and went not down to his house.

10. And when they had told David, saying, Uriah went not down unto his house, David said unto

Uriah, Camest thou not from thy journey? why then didst thou not go down unto thine house?

11. And Uriah said unto David, The ark, and Israel, and Judah, abide in tents; and my lord Joab, and the servants of my lord, are encamped in the open fields; shall I then go into mine house, to eat and to drink, and to lie with my wife? as thou livest, and as thy soul liveth, I will not do this thing.

12. And David said to Uriah, Tarry here to day also, and to morrow I will let thee depart. So Uriah abode in Jerusalem that day, and the morrow.

13. And when David had called him, he did eat and drink before him; and he made him drunk: and at even he went out to lie on his bed with the servants of his lord, but went not down to his house.

14. And it came to pass in the morning, that David wrote a letter to Joab, and sent it by the hand of Uriah.

15. And he wrote in the letter, saying, Set ye Uriah in the forefront of the hottest battle, and retire ye from him, that he may be smitten, and die.

16. And it came to pass, when Joab observed the city, that he assigned Uriah unto a place where he knew that valiant men were.

17. And the men of the city went out, and fought with Joab: and there fell some of the people of the servants of David; and Uriah the Hittite died also.

18. Then Joab sent and told David all the things concerning the war;

19. And charged the messenger, saying, When thou hast made an end of telling the matters of the war unto the king,

20. And if so be that the king's wrath arise, and he say unto thee, Wherefore approached ye so nigh unto the city when ye did fight? knew ye not that they would shoot from the wall?

21. Who smote Abimelech the son of Jerubbesheth? did not a woman cast a piece of a millstone upon him from the wall, that he died in

Thebez? why went ye nigh the wall? then say thou, Thy servant Uriah the Hittite is dead also.

22. So the messenger went, and came and shewed David all that Joab had sent him for.

23. And the messenger said unto David, Surely the men prevailed against us, and came out unto us into the field, and we were upon them even unto the entering of the gate.

24. And the shooters shot from off the wall upon thy servants; and some of the king's servants be dead, and thy servant Uriah the Hittite is dead also.

25. Then David said unto the messenger, Thus shalt thou say unto Joab, Let not this thing displease thee, for the sword devoureth one as well as another: make thy battle more strong against the city, and overthrow it: and encourage thou him.

26. And when the wife of Uriah heard that Uriah her husband was dead, she mourned for her husband.

27. And when the mourning was past, David sent and fetched her to his house, and she became his

wife, and bare him a son. But the thing that David had done displeased the Lord.

Parable of the Prodigal Son – Luke 15:11-32

11. And he said, A certain man had two sons:

12. And the younger of them said to his father, Father, give me the portion of goods that falleth to me. And he divided unto them his living.

13. And not many days after the younger son gathered all together, and took his journey into a far country, and there wasted his substance with riotous living.

14. And when he had spent all, there arose a mighty famine in that land; and he began to be in want.

15. And he went and joined himself to a citizen of that country; and he sent him into his fields to feed swine.

16. And he would fain have filled his belly with the husks that the swine did eat: and no man gave unto him.

17. And when he came to himself, he said, How many hired servants of my father's have bread enough and to spare, and I perish with hunger!

18. I will arise and go to my father, and will say unto him, Father, I have sinned against heaven, and before thee,

19. And am no more worthy to be called thy son: make me as one of thy hired servants.

20. And he arose, and came to his father. But when he was yet a great way off, his father saw him, and had compassion, and ran, and fell on his neck, and kissed him.

21. And the son said unto him, Father, I have sinned against heaven, and in thy sight, and am no more worthy to be called thy son.

22. But the father said to his servants, Bring forth

the best robe, and put it on him; and put a ring on his hand, and shoes on his feet:

23. And bring hither the fatted calf, and kill it; and let us eat, and be merry:

24. For this my son was dead, and is alive again; he was lost, and is found. And they began to be merry.

25. Now his elder son was in the field: and as he came and drew nigh to the house, he heard musick and dancing.

26. And he called one of the servants, and asked what these things meant.

27. And he said unto him, Thy brother is come; and thy father hath killed the fatted calf, because he hath received him safe and sound.

28. And he was angry, and would not go in: therefore came his father out, and entreated him.

29. And he answering said to his father, Lo, these many years do I serve thee, neither transgressed I at any time thy commandment: and yet thou never

gavest me a kid, that I might make merry with my friends:

30. But as soon as this thy son was come, which hath devoured thy living with harlots, thou hast killed for him the fatted calf.

31. And he said unto him, Son, thou art ever with me, and all that I have is thine.

32. It was meet that we should make merry, and be glad: for this thy brother was dead, and is alive again; and was lost, and is found.

Parable of the Pharisee and the Publican – Luke 18:9-14

9. And he spake this parable unto certain which trusted in themselves that they were righteous, and despised others:

10. Two men went up into the temple to pray; the one a Pharisee, and the other a publican.

11. The Pharisee stood and prayed thus with himself, God, I thank thee, that I am not as other

men are, extortioners, unjust, adulterers, or even as this publican.

12. I fast twice in the week, I give tithes of all that I possess.

13. And the publican, standing afar off, would not lift up so much as his eyes unto heaven, but smote upon his breast, saying, God be merciful to me a sinner.

14. I tell you, this man went down to his house justified rather than the other: for every one that exalteth himself shall be abased; and he that humbleth himself shall be exalted.

SECTION 2 – THE FLESH

The Fall of Man – Genesis 3:1-13

1. Now the serpent was more subtle than any beast of the field which the Lord God had made. And he said unto the woman, Yea, hath God said, Ye shall not eat of every tree of the garden?

2. And the woman said unto the serpent, We may eat of the fruit of the trees of the garden:

3. But of the fruit of the tree which is in the midst of the garden, God hath said, Ye shall not eat of it, neither shall ye touch it, lest ye die.

4. And the serpent said unto the woman, Ye shall not surely die:

5. For God doth know that in the day ye eat thereof, then your eyes shall be opened, and ye shall be as gods, knowing good and evil.

6. And when the woman saw that the tree was good for food, and that it was pleasant to the eyes, and a tree to be desired to make one wise, she took of the fruit thereof, and did eat, and gave also unto her husband with her; and he did eat.

7. And the eyes of them both were opened, and they knew that they were naked; and they sewed fig leaves together, and made themselves aprons.

8. And they heard the voice of the Lord God walking in the garden in the cool of the day: and Adam and his wife hid themselves from the presence of the Lord God amongst the trees of the garden.

9. And the Lord God called unto Adam, and said unto him, Where art thou?

10. And he said, I heard thy voice in the garden, and I was afraid, because I was naked; and I hid myself.

11. And he said, Who told thee that thou wast naked? Hast thou eaten of the tree, whereof I commanded thee that thou shouldest not eat?

12. And the man said, The woman whom thou gavest to be with me, she gave me of the tree, and I did eat.

13. And the Lord God said unto the woman, What is this that thou hast done? And the woman said, The serpent beguiled me, and I did eat.

Disciples and the Possessed Boy – Mark 9:17-30

17. And one of the multitude answered and said, Master, I have brought unto thee my son, which hath a dumb spirit;

18. And wheresoever he taketh him, he teareth him: and he foameth, and gnasheth with his teeth, and pineth away: and I spake to thy disciples that they should cast him out; and they could not.

19. He answereth him, and saith, O faithless generation, how long shall I be with you? how long shall I suffer you? bring him unto me.

20. And they brought him unto him: and when he saw him, straightway the spirit tare him; and he fell on the ground, and wallowed foaming.

21. And he asked his father, How long is it ago since this came unto him? And he said, Of a child.

22. And oft times it hath cast him into the fire, and into the waters, to destroy him: but if thou canst do any thing, have compassion on us, and help us.

23. Jesus said unto him, If thou canst believe, all things are possible to him that believeth.

24. And straightway the father of the child cried out, and said with tears, Lord, I believe; help thou mine unbelief.

25. When Jesus saw that the people came running together, he rebuked the foul spirit, saying unto him, Thou dumb and deaf spirit, I charge thee, come out of him, and enter no more into him.

26. And the spirit cried, and rent him sore, and came out of him: and he was as one dead; insomuch that many said, He is dead.

27. But Jesus took him by the hand, and lifted him up; and he arose.

28. And when he was come into the house, his disciples asked him privately, Why could not we cast him out?

29. And he said unto them, This kind can come forth by nothing, but by prayer and fasting.

30. And they departed thence, and passed through Galilee; and he would not that any man should know it.

SECTION 3 – THE DEVIL

David & Ziklag – I Samuel 29:1-11, 30:1-6

1. Now the Philistines gathered together all their armies to Aphek: and the Israelites pitched by a fountain which is in Jezreel.

2. And the lords of the Philistines passed on by hundreds, and by thousands: but David and his men passed on in the rearward with Achish.

3. Then said the princes of the Philistines, What do these Hebrews here? And Achish said unto the princes of the Philistines, Is not this David, the servant of Saul the king of Israel, which hath been with me these days, or these years, and I have found no fault in him since he fell unto me unto this day?

4. And the princes of the Philistines were wroth with him; and the princes of the Philistines said unto him, Make this fellow return, that he may go again to his place which thou hast appointed him, and let him not go down with us to battle, lest in the battle he be an adversary to us: for wherewith should he reconcile himself unto his master? should it not be with the heads of these men?

5. Is not this David, of whom they sang one to another in dances, saying, Saul slew his thousands, and David his ten thousands?

6. Then Achish called David, and said unto him, Surely, as the Lord liveth, thou hast been upright, and thy going out and thy coming in with me in the host is good in my sight: for I have not found evil in thee since the day of thy coming unto me unto this day: nevertheless the lords favour thee not.

7. Wherefore now return, and go in peace, that thou displease not the lords of the Philistines.

8. And David said unto Achish, But what have I done? and what hast thou found in thy servant so

long as I have been with thee unto this day, that I may not go fight against the enemies of my lord the king?

9. And Achish answered and said to David, I know that thou art good in my sight, as an angel of God: notwithstanding the princes of the Philistines have said, He shall not go up with us to the battle.

10. Wherefore now rise up early in the morning with thy master's servants that are come with thee: and as soon as ye be up early in the morning, and have light, depart.

11. So David and his men rose up early to depart in the morning, to return into the land of the Philistines. And the Philistines went up to Jezreel.

Chapter 30

1. And it came to pass, when David and his men were come to Ziklag on the third day, that the Amalekites had invaded the south, and Ziklag, and smitten Ziklag, and burned it with fire;

2. And had taken the women captives, that were therein: they slew not any, either great or small, but carried them away, and went on their way.

3. So David and his men came to the city, and, behold, it was burned with fire; and their wives, and their sons, and their daughters, were taken captives.

4. Then David and the people that were with him lifted up their voice and wept, until they had no more power to weep.

5. And David's two wives were taken captives, Ahinoam the Jezreelitess, and Abigail the wife of Nabal the Carmelite.

6. And David was greatly distressed; for the people spake of stoning him, because the soul of all the people was grieved, every man for his sons and for his daughters: but David encouraged himself in the Lord his God.

The Sadducees test Jesus – Mark 12:18-27

18. Then come unto him the Sadducees, which say there is no resurrection; and they asked him, saying,

19. Master, Moses wrote unto us, If a man's brother die, and leave his wife behind him, and leave no children, that his brother should take his wife, and raise up seed unto his brother.

20. Now there were seven brethren: and the first took a wife, and dying left no seed.

21. And the second took her, and died, neither left he any seed: and the third likewise.

22. And the seven had her, and left no seed: last of all the woman died also.

23. In the resurrection therefore, when they shall rise, whose wife shall she be of them? for the seven had her to wife.

24. And Jesus answering said unto them, Do ye not therefore err, because ye know not the scriptures, neither the power of God?

25. For when they shall rise from the dead, they neither marry, nor are given in marriage; but are as the angels which are in heaven.

26. And as touching the dead, that they rise: have ye not read in the book of Moses, how in the bush God spake unto him, saying, I am the God of Abraham, and the God of Isaac, and the God of Jacob?

27. He is not the God of the dead, but the God of the living: ye therefore do greatly err.

Parable of Farmer & Seed – Matthew 13:1-9; 18-23

1. The same day went Jesus out of the house, and sat by the sea side.

2. And great multitudes were gathered together unto him, so that he went into a ship, and sat; and the whole multitude stood on the shore.

3. And he spake many things unto them in parables, saying, Behold, a sower went forth to sow;

4. And when he sowed, some seeds fell by the way side, and the fowls came and devoured them up:

5. Some fell upon stony places, where they had not much earth: and forthwith they sprung up, because they had no deepness of earth:

6. And when the sun was up, they were scorched; and because they had no root, they withered away.

7. And some fell among thorns; and the thorns sprung up, and choked them:

8. But other fell into good ground, and brought forth fruit, some an hundredfold, some sixtyfold, some thirtyfold.

9. Who hath ears to hear, let him hear.

Hear ye therefore the parable of the sower.

19.   When any one heareth the word of the kingdom, and understandeth it not, then cometh the wicked one, and catcheth away that which was sown in his heart. This is he which received seed by the way side.

20.   But he that received the seed into stony places, the same is he that heareth the word, and anon with joy receiveth it;

21.   Yet hath he not root in himself, but dureth for a while: for when tribulation or persecution ariseth because of the word, by and by he is offended.

22.   He also that received seed among the thorns is he that heareth the word; and the care of this world, and the deceitfulness of riches, choke the word, and he becometh unfruitful.

23.   But he that received seed into the good ground is he that heareth the word, and understandeth it; which also beareth fruit, and bringeth forth, some an hundredfold, some sixty, some thirty.

Jehoshaphat against Three Nations – II Chronicles 20:1-28

1. It came to pass after this also, that the children of Moab, and the children of Ammon, and with them other beside the Ammonites, came against Jehoshaphat to battle.

2. Then there came some that told Jehoshaphat, saying, There cometh a great multitude against thee from beyond the sea on this side Syria; and, behold, they be in Hazazontamar, which is Engedi.

3. And Jehoshaphat feared, and set himself to seek the Lord, and proclaimed a fast throughout all Judah.

4. And Judah gathered themselves together, to ask help of the Lord: even out of all the cities of Judah they came to seek the Lord.

5. And Jehoshaphat stood in the congregation of Judah and Jerusalem, in the house of the Lord, before the new court,

6. And said, O Lord God of our fathers, art not

thou God in heaven? and rulest not thou over all the kingdoms of the heathen? and in thine hand is there not power and might, so that none is able to withstand thee?

7. Art not thou our God, who didst drive out the inhabitants of this land before thy people Israel, and gavest it to the seed of Abraham thy friend for ever?

8. And they dwelt therein, and have built thee a sanctuary therein for thy name, saying,

9. If, when evil cometh upon us, as the sword, judgment, or pestilence, or famine, we stand before this house, and in thy presence, (for thy name is in this house,) and cry unto thee in our affliction, then thou wilt hear and help.

10. And now, behold, the children of Ammon and Moab and mount Seir, whom thou wouldest not let Israel invade, when they came out of the land of Egypt, but they turned from them, and destroyed them not;

11. Behold, I say, how they reward us, to come to cast us out of thy possession, which thou hast given us to inherit.

12. O our God, wilt thou not judge them? for we have no might against this great company that cometh against us; neither know we what to do: but our eyes are upon thee.

13. And all Judah stood before the Lord, with their little ones, their wives, and their children.

14. Then upon Jahaziel the son Zechariah, the son of Benaiah, the son of Jeiel, the son of Mattaniah, a Levite of the sons of Asaph, came the Spirit of the Lord in the midst of the congregation;

15. And he said, Hearken ye, all Judah, and ye inhabitants of Jerusalem, and thou king Jehoshaphat, Thus saith the Lord unto you, Be not afraid nor dismayed by reason of this great multitude; for the battle is not yours, but God's.

16. To morrow go ye down against them: behold, they come up by the cliff of Ziz; and ye shall find them at the end of the brook, before the wilderness

of Jeruel.

17. Ye shall not need to fight in this battle: set yourselves, stand ye still, and see the salvation of the Lord with you, O Judah and Jerusalem: fear not, nor be dismayed; to morrow go out against them: for the Lord will be with you.

18. And Jehoshaphat bowed his head with his face to the ground: and all Judah and the inhabitants of Jerusalem fell before the Lord, worshipping the Lord.

19. And the Levites, of the children of the Kohathites, and of the children of the Korhites, stood up to praise the Lord God of Israel with a loud voice on high.

20. And they rose early in the morning, and went forth into the wilderness of Tekoa: and as they went forth, Jehoshaphat stood and said, Hear me, O Judah, and ye inhabitants of Jerusalem; Believe in the Lord your God, so shall ye be established; believe his prophets, so shall ye prosper.

21. And when he had consulted with the people, he appointed singers unto the Lord, and that should praise the beauty of holiness, as they went out before the army, and to say, Praise the Lord; for his mercy endureth for ever.

22. And when they began to sing and to praise, the Lord set ambushments against the children of Ammon, Moab, and mount Seir, which were come against Judah; and they were smitten.

23. For the children of Ammon and Moab stood up against the inhabitants of mount Seir, utterly to slay and destroy them: and when they had made an end of the inhabitants of Seir, every one helped to destroy another.

24. And when Judah came toward the watch tower in the wilderness, they looked unto the multitude, and, behold, they were dead bodies fallen to the earth, and none escaped.

25. And when Jehoshaphat and his people came to take away the spoil of them, they found among them in abundance both riches with the dead

bodies, and precious jewels, which they stripped off for themselves, more than they could carry away: and they were three days in gathering of the spoil, it was so much.

26.   And on the fourth day, they assembled themselves in the valley of Berachah; for there they blessed the Lord: therefore the name of the same place was called, The valley of Berachah, unto this day.

27.   Then they returned, every man of Judah and Jerusalem, and Jehoshaphat in the forefront of them, to go again to Jerusalem with joy; for the Lord had made them to rejoice over their enemies.

28.   And they came to Jerusalem with psalteries and harps and trumpets unto the house of the Lord.

Joshua at Jericho – Joshua 6:1-21

1. Now Jericho was straitly shut up because of the children of Israel: none went out, and none came in.

2.   And the Lord said unto Joshua, See, I have given into thine hand Jericho, and the king thereof, and the mighty men of valour.

3.   And ye shall compass the city, all ye men of war, and go round about the city once. Thus shalt thou do six days.

4.   And seven priests shall bear before the ark seven trumpets of rams' horns: and the seventh day ye shall compass the city seven times, and the priests shall blow with the trumpets.

5.   And it shall come to pass, that when they make a long blast with the ram's horn, and when ye hear the sound of the trumpet, all the people shall shout with a great shout; and the wall of the city shall fall down flat, and the people shall ascend up every man straight before him.

6.   And Joshua the son of Nun called the priests, and said unto them, Take up the ark of the covenant, and let seven priests bear seven trumpets of rams' horns before the ark of the Lord.

7.   And he said unto the people, Pass on, and compass the city, and let him that is armed pass on before the ark of the Lord.

8.   And it came to pass, when Joshua had spoken unto the people, that the seven priests bearing the seven trumpets of rams' horns passed on before the Lord, and blew with the trumpets: and the ark of the covenant of the Lord followed them.

9.   And the armed men went before the priests that blew with the trumpets, and the rearward came after the ark, the priests going on, and blowing with the trumpets.

10.   And Joshua had commanded the people, saying, Ye shall not shout, nor make any noise with your voice, neither shall any word proceed out of your mouth, until the day I bid you shout; then shall ye shout.

11.   So the ark of the Lord compassed the city, going about it once: and they came into the camp, and lodged in the camp.

12. And Joshua rose early in the morning, and the priests took up the ark of the Lord.

13. And seven priests bearing seven trumpets of rams' horns before the ark of the Lord went on continually, and blew with the trumpets: and the armed men went before them; but the rereward came after the ark of the Lord, the priests going on, and blowing with the trumpets.

14. And the second day they compassed the city once, and returned into the camp: so they did six days.

15. And it came to pass on the seventh day, that they rose early about the dawning of the day, and compassed the city after the same manner seven times: only on that day they compassed the city seven times.

16. And it came to pass at the seventh time, when the priests blew with the trumpets, Joshua said unto the people, Shout; for the Lord hath given you the city.

17. And the city shall be accursed, even it, and all

that are therein, to the Lord: only Rahab the harlot shall live, she and all that are with her in the house, because she hid the messengers that we sent.

18. And ye, in any wise keep yourselves from the accursed thing, lest ye make yourselves accursed, when ye take of the accursed thing, and make the camp of Israel a curse, and trouble it.

19. But all the silver, and gold, and vessels of brass and iron, are consecrated unto the Lord: they shall come into the treasury of the Lord.

20. So the people shouted when the priests blew with the trumpets: and it came to pass, when the people heard the sound of the trumpet, and the people shouted with a great shout, that the wall fell down flat, so that the people went up into the city, every man straight before him, and they took the city.

21. And they utterly destroyed all that was in the city, both man and woman, young and old, and ox, and sheep, and ass, with the edge of the sword.

Paul and Silas at Philippi – Acts 16:12-26

12. And from thence to Philippi, which is the chief city of that part of Macedonia, and a colony: and we were in that city abiding certain days.

13. And on the Sabbath we went out of the city by a river side, where prayer was wont to be made; and we sat down, and spake unto the women which resorted thither.

14. And a certain woman named Lydia, a seller of purple, of the city of Thyatira, which worshipped God, heard us: whose heart the Lord opened, that she attended unto the things which were spoken of Paul.

15. And when she was baptized, and her household, she besought us, saying, If ye have judged me to be faithful to the Lord, come into my house, and abide there. And she constrained us.

16. And it came to pass, as we went to prayer, a certain damsel possessed with a spirit of divination

met us, which brought her masters much gain by soothsaying:

17. The same followed Paul and us, and cried, saying, These men are the servants of the most high God, which shew unto us the way of salvation.

18. And this did she many days. But Paul, being grieved, turned and said to the spirit, I command thee in the name of Jesus Christ to come out of her. And he came out the same hour.

19. And when her masters saw that the hope of their gains was gone, they caught Paul and Silas, and drew them into the marketplace unto the rulers,

20. And brought them to the magistrates, saying, These men, being Jews, do exceedingly trouble our city,

21. And teach customs, which are not lawful for us to receive, neither to observe, being Romans.

22.   And the multitude rose up together against them: and the magistrates rent off their clothes, and commanded to beat them.

23.   And when they had laid many stripes upon them, they cast them into prison, charging the jailor to keep them safely:

24.   Who, having received such a charge, thrust them into the inner prison, and made their feet fast in the stocks.

25.   And at midnight Paul and Silas prayed, and sang praises unto God: and the prisoners heard them.

26.   And suddenly there was a great earthquake, so that the foundations of the prison were shaken: and immediately all the doors were opened, and every one's bands were loosed.

Bibliography

Lockman Foundation. *Comparative Study Bible.*
Zondervan Publishing House. Grand Rapids,
MI, c1984

The Bible Library. *The Bible Library CD Rom
Disc.* Ellis Enterprises Incorporated, (c)
1988 – 2000. 4205 McAuley Blvd., Suite
385, Oklahoma City, OK 73120. All Rights
Reserved.

www.ingramcontent.com/pod-product-compliance
Lightning Source LLC
Chambersburg PA
CBHW030759150426

42813CB00068B/3253/J